Emotionally Unstable Mumma: From Broken to Blessed – A Survivor's Story of Dunblane, Trauma and Healing

Amy Rose

Copyright © 2012 Amy Rose

All rights reserved.

ISBN: 9798289901828

DEDICATION

To Ryan —

You walked into my life when my world was at its messiest, and you stayed. Thank you for loving me through the chaos, for seeing the woman behind the wounds, and for reminding me every single day that I am worthy of peace, love, and happiness. Your patience, your presence, and your quiet strength have held me up more times than you'll ever know.

To my children —

You are my heart outside my body. Everything I've done, everything I've fought through, has been with you in mind. Your laughter, your resilience, and your love have carried me through my darkest moments. I hope one day you'll understand how deeply you've saved me, simply by being mine. This story is as much yours as it is mine.

To my family and friends —

To those who have stood by me through the storm — thank you for holding space for my pain, for celebrating my healing, and for never letting go when I felt like falling. Whether you offered a listening ear, a warm cup of tea, or a simple message of encouragement, know that it mattered more than words can say.

This book is for all of you —

For the ones who never stopped believing I could rise from the ashes.

CONTENTS

	Acknowledgments	i
1	Introduction	1
2	An Emotionally Unstable Personality	Pg 6
3	Becoming Emotionally Unstable	Pg 18
4	Growing Up Emotionally Unstable	Pg 31
5	An Emotionally Unstable Marriage	Pg 48
6	An Emotionally Unstable Ending	Pg 77
7	Emotionally Unstable True Love	Pg 90
8	Emotionally Unstable New Beginnings	Pg 106
9	Emotionally Stable New Beginnings?	Pg 138
	Epilogue	Pg 152

ACKNOWLEDGMENTS

There are people who help put the pieces back together when everything feels broken. This book — this dream — wouldn't exist without you.

To my darling Dad —
Thank you for loving me so consistently, for supporting me endlessly, and for always being there, no matter what. Your quiet strength and unwavering belief in me have been a constant in my life. I am so proud to be your daughter — and I always will be.

To Carl and Debbie —
Thank you for saving my life. Your support, honesty, and guidance gave me the tools I needed to keep going. I wouldn't be here without you.

To everyone who donated to my fundraiser —
Thank you for helping turn a long-held dream into reality. Your generosity made this possible.

To the lovely Lynn —
Thank you for being a constant source of encouragement and kindness.

To the beautiful Zara —
Your energy and support have lifted me more than you know.

To the wonderful Connor William —
Thank you for believing in me and cheering me on when I needed it most.

To Sharon and Andy —
You are everything anyone could hope for in in-laws. Thank you for your love, your support, and your belief in me. I'm so lucky to have you both.

To the best brother-in-law, Shaun —
Thank you for your quiet strength, your steady presence, and your kind heart. You've always made me feel welcome and accepted, and your gentle way of showing up means more than you probably realise.

To my awesome Godmother Jude —
Thank you for loving me, believing in me, and always making me feel like I matter. Your support has meant the world to me.

To my school friend Megan —Over 20 years of friendship, and your love and loyalty have never wavered. I'm so grateful for you.

Thank you all. This story may be mine, but it was made possible by you.

PART 1 - INTRODUCTION

- **My reason for writing this book**

Hi, I'm Amy.

I may not call myself an author in the traditional sense, but I am a storyteller. I have lived a life filled with struggles, traumas, and triumphs—and now I'm sharing that story with you. My hope is that in these pages, you'll find something that resonates, something that brings you hope, or even a sense of connection.

My sole reason for writing this book and so publicly airing my struggles, traumas and newly found wellbeing is in the hope that it helps even one person not to lose hope even in their darkest hours. I pray that these words reach those who need them and that others are encouraged to keep going no matter what challenges they're facing or what has happened in their past. There is nothing in this world that is more important to me than loving and helping others, in any way I can, and if telling my own story does that then I have achieved my objective.

It's a long story, 38 years' worth to be precise. Some amazing, some awful and some in between and just plain ordinary. I'm going to take you on a journey from the beginning and go through some of the most pertinent events in my life. While I understand that many people in this world endure unimaginable suffering, this is my story. It is not a comparison of pain, but an honest account of my own journey.

- **Trigger warnings**

Before we begin, I must give you some trigger warnings. My story includes sensitive topics, including trauma, abuse, and mental health struggles. Please take care of yourself as you read on. These are my lived experiences, and they have shaped me in ways that I will explain throughout the book.

I had one major trauma, as a child at Dunblane Primary School on the day of the massacre in 1996, which is a story I will tell from my perspective within this book, but there are a number of other factors that have fed into the emotional instabilities that I have experienced throughout my life. These include:

- Sexual Abuse
- Narcissistic Abuse
- Divorce
- Suicide Attempts
- Depression
- Anxiety
- Family Breakdown
- Self-Harm

If you want a real, raw and inspiring story, then I believe this is the book for you. I believe in talking openly about mental health and am acutely aware that sometimes it's the people you would never expect that are suffering more than you could ever imagine, in the hope that it encourages people to always be kind. It's said often, but it bears repeating: You never truly know what someone is going through. Everyone you meet will have some level of trauma, stress or emotional baggage that they are carrying with them, and kindness may be the only thing that keeps them going.

I've made mistakes in my past, and some of those actions still weigh on me today. But through it all, I've learned the importance of forgiveness—both for others and for myself. I own my mistakes and accept them as part of my journey, but I will not let them define me.

As you go through this book, this history of my life, I will share with you these mistakes and behaviours, and I hope that you are able to see that at the very core of who I know I am, is goodness. I love deeply, with everything within me, I will give love and support to anyone who needs it and I spend my life trying to ensure I make others feel good, happy and well supported.

However, not everyone that knows me will like me as they may only know stories of me and my behaviours in the past, I may have done wrong by them in some way or another and they have every right to hold on to that narrative of who I am. I'm not here to prove myself as some angel, I'm far from perfect and still have much to learn and a long way to go in life, however I do take responsibility for my actions, I get it wrong a lot, but I own my shit and will always do what I can to put things right. If I have ever done you wrong, please know from the bottom of my heart that I am sorry, I absolutely regret it and have undoubtedly punished myself for it over the years.

All I can do from this very moment moving forwards is be the best version of me that I have ever been for myself, for my family, my children and for humanity at large. It is my absolute intention to be authentically me throughout this book, to be completely honest and open with all of you that have taken the time to pick up and read my story and I can only pray that it reaches someone, somewhere that needs it and they come to realise that true beauty comes when you don't give up.

- **It's not just one trauma- the complexities involved**

So, as mentioned previously, I had one major trauma, a mass shooting at my school, just a few months before my 9th birthday which had a huge impact on my mental wellbeing, emotional state and how I viewed the world. My personality changed completely that day, I went from an outgoing, bubbly, confident little girl and became fearful, highly sensitive, emotional and lost in the world. I lost my trust in people, my faith in anything good and no longer knew who I was or what the purpose of me being here was. I felt guilty that I had survived when such young, innocent lives had been lost.

However, there are other complexities involved in my story that have had equally as big an impact on me and my mental health. As you can probably tell from the list of trigger warnings, my life has been a rollercoaster ride of emotions from the start, with lots of wonderful highs yet some deep and dark lows. As you go through this book I will share with you some of the most impactful times in my life as I went from a traumatised child and found my way in the world of adulthood.

- **The light at the end of the tunnel**

It's not all doom and gloom I promise. While my journey has been filled with deep struggles, I stand before you today, a testament to what's possible on the other side of pain. It's true that I've faced dark times—but I've also found light, love, and the kind of peace I never thought possible. I am incredibly happily settled down with my soul mate, Ryan, who has shown me the true meaning of unconditional love. Together we are blessed with the gift of raising 3 beautiful, happy, healthy children. For that I couldn't possibly be more grateful, I appreciate every single day just how blessed I am to have the love of my family, to be a mother, a partner, a daughter, a sister and a friend. I have my tribe of people I love more than life itself and for them I am eternally grateful. Through the love and support of others I have been able to find myself, my interests, my passions and a deep sense of self love and worth.

I must also acknowledge the generosity I've received throughout my life, from many sources—without which, I may not have the life I do today. My greatest gift, though, is emotional stability —the ability to live with self-awareness and peace, despite everything I've been through. It wasn't always easy, but thanks to the love of my family and the support I've received, I have a life today that's filled with joy and stability. Be it friends, family, colleagues, or professionals including the NHS Psychiatrist who finally heard me and found the right medication for me or the range of different therapists I have spoken to and seen throughout my adult life. Every single one of them has played a key part in me becoming who I am today. There are a couple of therapists I will speak of specifically in this book, as what they did I can only describe as true magic, however I am equally grateful to anyone and everyone that has been a part of some or all of this journey with me.

PART 2 - AN EMOTIONALLY UNSTABLE PERSONALITY

- **Emotional Instability and Me**

I want to be completely transparent from the beginning and share that I don't have a formal diagnosis, though I exhibit emotionally unstable traits. My former psychiatrist didn't deem my condition severe enough for an Emotionally Unstable Personality Disorder diagnosis. He told me, with unsettling honesty, that fifty percent of psychiatrists would label me, and fifty percent would not. That ambiguous assessment left me feeling adrift—like I was stuck somewhere between "normal" and "unwell," never quite belonging to either world. It felt like my pain didn't count unless it could be categorised, and for a long time, I internalised that confusion. I questioned myself constantly—was I just too sensitive? Was I overreacting? Was it all in my head?

Even though I can hold down a job and maintain long-term friendships and relationships, it often comes at a price that few can see. These connections require enormous amounts of effort—patience, self-monitoring, and a constant inner battle to stay regulated. I've learned to apologise more quickly, to pull back when I feel the urge to lash out, to try and name the emotion before it swallows me whole. But it's exhausting. Some days, just being 'normal' feels like a performance I barely hold together.

The truth is, I feel things more deeply than most people seem to. A casual comment can haunt me for days. Rejection, even imagined, can send me into a spiral. I've sat in rooms full of people feeling completely alone, convinced I was too much, or not enough, or somehow both at the same time. There have been moments when I couldn't trust my own thoughts—when the emotional intensity drowned out logic, and shame followed close behind like a shadow I couldn't outrun.

Medication has helped—it's steadied me. It hasn't numbed me, which was my biggest fear, but instead it's like someone finally gave me the remote control to the volume on my emotions. The storm still comes, but now I have an umbrella. I still struggle—some days more than others—but the difference is, I'm not constantly bracing for emotional impact anymore. There's space between the feeling and the reaction. And that space has changed everything.

I still live with depression and anxiety—they're like background music I've learned to tune out most days—but they no longer control the tempo of my life. I've spent years developing self-awareness, clawing my way out of patterns that used to define me. I've hurt people I love with my outbursts and silences. I've burned bridges and rebuilt them, not always successfully. But I've also grown. I've learned to soften. To pause. To forgive myself.

I'm not perfect. I still break down. I still have moments where the past creeps in and whispers old lies. But I am no longer lost in the chaos of my emotions. I am learning to live alongside them—to understand them, to hold them gently, rather than fear them. And that, for me, is what healing looks like. I'm proud to say that I am now stable and well—most of the time. And for someone like me, "most of the time" is a quiet, beautiful victory

- **How it affects me**

For me, emotional instability has never been a neat, clinical definition on a page—it's been a lived reality, loud and chaotic, brutal and suffocating. It can manifest in endless ways. Some mornings, I would wake up and instantly sense the unpredictability of the day ahead. I wouldn't know if I could tolerate being around others—or even being alone with myself. At times, I'd feel inexplicably angry, the rage bubbling under my skin without a nameable source. Other days, I'd cry for hours on end, sobbing for reasons I couldn't articulate, as if my body remembered a pain my mind couldn't locate.

There were moments of spontaneous joy too—singing loudly in the car, dancing while driving, feeling alive in a way that made me believe I was finally okay. But then I'd come home, shut the door, and be instantly crushed by a wave of exhaustion and despair. The contrast was jarring: lightness to darkness in an instant. I'd collapse under the weight of daily responsibilities, unable to cook a meal, answer a message, or even take a shower. I'd shut down completely, as if my nervous system had blown a fuse.

Sometimes, the trigger was subtle—a smell, a tone of voice, a look—something that stirred up old wounds I didn't even realise were still bleeding. Suddenly, I was no longer in the present moment; I was back in the past, reliving pain I had buried. Emotional instability often meant believing that every word, every action from others was aimed at me—an unspoken judgment, a withdrawal of love. If my partner didn't say "I love you too" at the end of a call, I wouldn't just feel sad. I would break. I'd sit on the floor sobbing; absolutely certain he didn't love me the way I loved him. That he was pulling away, that I was too much, not enough, a burden.

Other times, it would escalate quickly—a disagreement, a criticism, a misunderstanding—and I would spiral. I'd hide away, consumed by overwhelming shame and distress, hurting myself in terrifying, visceral ways: smashing my head against the floor, tearing clumps of hair from my scalp, dragging my nails across my face until it bled. Years ago, when things were at their worst, I remember picking up a bread knife in a state of pure panic and emotional chaos, trying to cut through my own arm—desperate to escape the storm inside me. There have been moments where I've genuinely wanted to die—not because I didn't want to live, but because I didn't know how to survive the pain.

These behaviours weren't about attention. They were the only ways I had ever learned to release the unbearable tension in my body and mind. The thoughts felt erratic, irrational, deafening—and the pain demanded a physical outlet. It was also punishment: for not being better, for not being able to hold it all together, for disappointing the people around me. I knew the way I reacted wasn't okay. I hated myself for it. But knowing and stopping were two very different things.

All the while, I wore a mask. I lived a high-functioning life—worked hard, kept up appearances, smiled on cue—while hiding an internal chaos that few could have imagined. I was terrified of people seeing the real me. Terrified of being unmasked and exposed. The truth is, only a handful of people have ever seen me at my lowest, and even they haven't witnessed the full extent of the darkness I've endured. Before I began speaking openly about my mental health, almost no one in my life had any idea of what I'd been through, or how close I'd come to the edge.

At times, the pendulum would swing in the opposite direction. I'd feel euphoric, inspired, electric with energy. I'd start planning new businesses, booking spontaneous holidays, calling friends I hadn't spoken to in years, making grand plans for adventures I couldn't afford. I'd express endless love, buy extravagant gifts I couldn't financially sustain, and convince myself I had finally "cracked" the code to happiness. I became everyone's go-to—therapist, cleaner, dog-sitter, organiser, life coach—spinning in a blur of optimism and purpose. But eventually, the crash would come, leaving me buried in debt, emotionally drained, and once again ashamed.

There were times I became so anxious I couldn't leave the house, not even to visit a local shop. I'd avoid answering the door, terrified of unexpected contact. Other times, I became overbearing and hyper, my behaviour becoming performative, clown-like—seeking validation through exaggerated cheerfulness, only to later drown in shame. I remember being at friend's children's birthday parties, completely unable to speak to people I'd known for decades. I'd shut down, barely holding back tears, longing to disappear.

Every emotion was all-consuming. Love so intense it became painful, suffocating. Fear so irrational it felt real. Anxiety so paralysing I couldn't go downstairs in my own home. Before I found the right medication and had access to therapy that truly helped, this was my reality *every single day*. It wasn't a bad mood or a rough patch—it was a relentless, merciless cycle. And it was utterly exhausting. It felt like living in a constant emotional hurricane, with no shelter in sight.

And yet, I learned. Slowly. Painfully. I began to understand myself. I began to build the tools to weather the storms inside me. Step by step, I started climbing out of the chaos.

Still, very few people knew any of this—because I never let them see it. Somewhere along the line, I had learned to hide my pain. To smile in public and scream in private. To meet every expectation placed upon me, even if it meant sacrificing my mental health. Maybe it was how I was raised. Maybe it was just what life taught me. But I became an expert at bottling up the big, unbearable feelings until I was alone. And then—then, they exploded.

Sometimes, the release was devastating. I could go from a seemingly normal day at work to coming home and attempting to hang myself in the garage. That's not an exaggeration—that's a truth I carry. And one I will share in time.

Is this what emotional instability looks like for others? I honestly don't know. I haven't lived their lives. I don't hear their thoughts or feel their pain. But if I had to guess, I'd say it's a rollercoaster for everyone who lives it. Overwhelming. Confusing. Frustrating. Lonely. And entirely individual. It's an illness that still carries far too much stigma, and it's painfully misunderstood—even by those who claim to understand it best.

I know firsthand that emotional instability can push people away, even those who love you. It can be too much. Too intense. Too consuming. Even the people who say they've researched your condition and "get it" may reach their breaking point. And that's what makes it all the more isolating. You're already lost inside your own mind—and then you're left to face it alone.

- **The real definition**

As for the official description of Emotionally Unstable Personality Disorder (or Borderline Personality Disorder as it is also commonly known) I will leave it to the medical experts, our wonderful National Health Service, who state;

'[1]Borderline personality disorder (BPD) is a disorder of mood and how a person interacts with others. It's the most commonly recognised personality

---

[1] https://www.nhs.uk/mental-health/conditions/borderline-personality-disorder/overview/#:~:text=Borderline%20personality%20disorder%20(BPD)%20is,most%20commonly%20recognised%20personality%20disorder.

disorder.

In general, someone with a personality disorder will differ significantly from an average person in terms of how he or she thinks, perceives, feels or relates to others.

Symptoms of borderline personality disorder (BPD)

The symptoms of BPD can be grouped into 4 main areas:

- emotional instability – the psychological term for this is affective dysregulation
- disturbed patterns of thinking or perception – cognitive distortions or perceptual distortions
- impulsive behaviour
- intense but unstable relationships with others

The symptoms of a personality disorder may range from mild to severe and usually emerge in adolescence, persisting into adulthood.

Causes of borderline personality disorder (BPD)

The causes of BPD are unclear. But as with most conditions, BPD appears to result from a combination of genetic and environmental factors.

People with BPD come from many different backgrounds, but most will have experienced some kind of trauma or neglect as children.

When to get medical advice

If you're experiencing symptoms of BPD, make an appointment with a GP.

They may ask about:

how you feel

your recent behaviour

what sort of impact your symptoms have had on your quality of life

This is to rule out other more common mental health conditions, such as depression, and to make sure there's no immediate risk to your health and wellbeing.

You may also find www.mind.co.uk a useful website.'

- **The Unseen Struggle**

My aim in sharing my story is to offer a window into the often-misunderstood world of emotional instability—to give voice to the silent storms so many of us endure. Whether someone has a formal diagnosis or not, the pain, confusion, and overwhelming emotional experiences are just as real, just as valid. I write this with the deepest sincerity: we are not abusive, irrational, or aggressive people by nature. We are, in truth, deeply empathetic, incredibly sensitive, and emotionally rich individuals whose minds simply process the world a little differently. Our intentions are rarely to harm, yet the intensity of our emotions can sometimes create unintended consequences. And for those moments—when I have hurt others, when my pain spilled outwards instead of staying contained—I carry a heavy burden of guilt. I never meant to hurt anyone. All I ever wanted was to be loved, to feel safe, and to protect those around me from the chaos within me. Yet I know I have caused pain, and I am deeply, achingly sorry.

For most of my early life, I didn't even realise I was unwell. I thought I was just "too much"—too sensitive, too emotional, too outspoken, too reactive. I often felt like I was fundamentally broken in a way that made me hard to love. I blamed myself for every emotional outburst, every misunderstanding, every distance that grew between me and the people I cared about. When I reflect on it now, I realise how young I was when it all began. I experienced a life-altering trauma at just eight years old, and though I couldn't comprehend it at the time, that was when the cracks in my emotional foundation started to form. But that trauma was only one part of the puzzle—there were many layers of pain, fear, and confusion that compounded over the years and shaped how I interacted with the world.

The first time I truly questioned my emotional wellbeing was at 22, when my now ex-husband—who had strong narcissistic traits—told me coldly that I was "not normal," that no one else would ever put up with my behaviour. And while I now recognise that this was as much about control as it was about truth, part of his words did land deeply. I could no longer ignore the fact that my emotional reactions didn't seem to match what I saw in others. I wasn't just struggling—I was suffering. But in my family, mental health wasn't something we talked about. I was loved, yes. I was hugged when I cried. But I was also quietly expected to "pull myself together." There was little room for messy emotions. When I became too dysregulated, I was shamed, dismissed, or told I was overreacting. I internalised that message: that I was wrong, defective, too much. And so, I tried harder and harder to hide how I felt, until it became second nature.

In my early twenties, I eventually saw a GP and was prescribed antidepressants. I was beginning to piece together what depression might look like for me, and how deeply it had sunk its claws into my everyday life. But I didn't fully understand it—and I certainly didn't have the tools to manage it. I drifted in and out of treatment, starting medication when things became unbearable, and stopping when I felt a bit more stable—only to crash again months later. It became a cycle I couldn't break. I lost the ability to work for months at a time, lost friendships, family connections. I stopped going out. I isolated myself. I was drowning in silence and shame, feeling completely alone and utterly broken.

All of this was further complicated by my toxic relationship with my ex-husband—a relationship that eroded what little self-worth I had left. His words, his gaslighting, his emotional manipulation chipped away at me until I barely recognised myself. But that's a chapter for later.

For now, what I want you to know is this: behind every "too much" person is usually someone who feels like not enough. Behind every emotional outburst is a sea of unspoken pain. And behind every apology, like the ones I carry in my heart every day, is a person just trying to make sense of themselves in a world that never taught them how.

- **Finally Seeing Me**

It wasn't until my 30s that I truly began to see myself — not the version I had masked and managed for so many years, but the raw, honest truth of who I was beneath the surface chaos. I stumbled across a Facebook post one evening, shared by an old work friend, about Emotionally Unstable Personality Disorder (EUPD). Her daughter had been diagnosed, and as I read through the symptoms and descriptions, something inside me shifted. It was like reading a detailed account of my own inner world — the intensity, the pain, the impulsiveness, the terrifying depth of emotions. I handed my phone to Ryan, and he said without hesitation, "That's you." His words struck a chord so deep that for a moment, I couldn't speak. My whole life began to make sense.

I wasn't a bad person. I wasn't broken beyond repair. I was unwell. I had always been unwell — misunderstood, misjudged, and drowning in emotions I never had the tools to explain or control. That night, I fell down a rabbit hole of research. I stayed up reading story after story of people who had lived through what I was living. And for the first time in years, I felt less alone. There was a name for this chaos — and with a name came hope.

The next morning, I made an appointment with my GP. I went in with trembling hands but a determined heart. I told them everything. Over the following months, I was referred to a psychiatrist who gently walked me through the assessment process. Though I didn't receive a formal diagnosis, the psychiatrist acknowledged that many of my emotional traits strongly mirrored EUPD. He prescribed me a low dose of mood stabilising, antipsychotic medication to complement the antidepressants I had been on for years. As the medication slowly took effect, a sense of calm began to emerge — fragile at first, like the first light after a storm — but real.

For the first time in my adult life, I wasn't just surviving the emotional extremes. I was managing them. The constant self-harm, the crippling shame, the rollercoaster relationships — they didn't disappear overnight, but they became quieter, less violent. My inner world, once filled with rage and panic, softened. I had space to breathe. I had clarity. I started to figure out who I actually was — beyond the chaos, beyond the pain — and for once, that version of me felt worthy of existing.

Over the past decade, I've explored various healing paths: talk therapy, Cognitive Behavioural Therapy, hypnotherapy, Integral Eye Movement Therapy. Every approach offered something — a sliver of insight, a tool for coping, a piece of the puzzle. But I was never deemed "unwell enough" to access Dialectical Behaviour Therapy (DBT) through the NHS. That still stings a little. DBT is something I continue to aspire toward privately, in the hope that one day I might be able to live medication-free — not because I'm ashamed of needing help, but because I long to trust my mind enough to stand on my own.

While I'm still walking the road of healing, I no longer feel lost on it. I have direction now. I understand my triggers. I no longer fear the tides of emotion that come and go — instead, I've learned to ride the waves. The day I recognised myself — truly saw myself in that Facebook post — was the day everything changed. I no longer see my emotions as my enemy, but as messengers. And with the right tools, patience, and support, I'm finally learning to listen.

PART 3 - BECOMING EMOTIONALLY UNSTABLE

- **The early days**

Like so many people, my earliest memories are not my own. They are fragments pieced together from stories told by others and faded photographs that capture moments I would never have remembered otherwise. Even those stories, handed down like fragile heirlooms, feel fragile themselves—some truths taught to me about my childhood now seem distorted, like shadows cast on a wall. This section attempts to untangle those shadows, to lay bare the tangled roots of my origins, and to sketch a preliminary portrait of who I am—and who I was meant to be.

I was born in 1987 in Leicestershire, the daughter of parents who still stood together then, but whose lives would unravel before I was even three. I have an older brother, two and a half years my senior—a constant figure in my early world. He was born with a lower limb disability and required a number of stays in hospital. Our grandparents, aunts, and uncle all lived close by, weaving a tight family web that seemed, from a child's eye, to hold us safe and warm. My mother often cared for cousins while my aunt worked, and I was shuffled between familiar houses, the comfort of grandparents' laps, the hum of family chatter. It felt like a typical working-class family, stitched together with love and routine.

My mum mostly stayed home, juggling part-time jobs, including at the University Library where my grandad was a professor. My dad's path shifted—from student to lecturer, working odd jobs to make ends meet. My brother's early years were marked by hospital visits and surgeries—his 'bad leg' a constant shadow, making his world smaller, quieter. My maternal grandparents became anchors for me during those times, holding me close when Mum was pulled between hospitals and home.

When my parents separated, I was too young to remember the split—but the story I grew up with painted my dad in dark, unforgiving strokes. A monster of a man, the narrative said—someone who screamed until we cowered in silence, who struck my brother so fiercely that his 'bad leg' bore the mark of a cruel hand for a week. A father who vanished from school events, who drank too much, who walked away from us without looking back. Some of the things said about him were so cruel, I can't even write them here.

But recently, I sought to listen differently, to hear other voices. I found my memories clashing against the stories—because my dad, in my heart, was not that man. I remember only one time he raised his voice—when I was thirteen, sneaking drinks at a family gathering. He told me to stop, simply, without anger or hate. Just a father trying to keep his daughter safe. Even when I blew up on him, and said awful things, he remained calm and consistent in his approach.

When I shared the darker stories with him years later, the pain in his eyes shattered something inside me. He looked broken, devastated to learn the weight of lies I had carried—lies that poisoned our connection, that explained the cold distance between us during my teenage years. His silence spoke volumes; beneath it lay a hurt I would never forget. His quiet suffering was a mirror to my own confusion and sorrow. I finally saw him—not as the villain I was told, but as a man hurt by misunderstandings and absence.

My dad is flawed, like all of us, but he is kind and generous, with a heart that quietly carries love. When I was four, I was moved more than 350 miles away, separated from him, and the chances for fatherhood were limited by distance. But he fought through the miles—weekly calls, school holidays filled with his efforts to be present. His love was steady, even if physically far.

I don't recall exactly when his long-term partner entered our lives, but I remember her kindness. She never forced herself on us, never demanded a place she wasn't given. As a teenager, I wanted to reject her, especially after overhearing my dad's affectionate pet name for her—a name once meant only for me. But her warmth broke down my walls. Now, both of them are part of my life, anchors for me and my children. My dad is not the angry, violent figure I was warned about—he is gentle, loving, and supportive in ways I hadn't dared to imagine.

After my parents' split, my mum moved into a new relationship with a man who had once been a friend to both my parents. We left Leicestershire behind and moved to Scotland when I was nearly five. The move uprooted us—350 miles away from everything I knew, from family and familiarity. Yet I adapted. I was outgoing, confident, and quickly made new friends. Highland dancing, Brownies, and endless days playing in the snowy parks filled those years with laughter and light.

My mum married my stepfather in a modest ceremony attended by their motorbike club friends. We spent four years in Scotland—years that remain some of the happiest of my life, despite the ache of distance from family. Visits from my stepsister and stepbrother brought joy, and trips back to England for family reunions were bittersweet, marked by laughter and the sting of goodbye. My childhood there was painted with freedom, friendship, and simple joys—long park days, school dances, snowstorms, motorbike rallies.

But my brother's experience was different. His disability kept him confined, unable to share the freedoms I enjoyed. My maternal grandparents lavished him with care, calling him 'their boy'—the only grandson in the family. I remember my grandmother's gentle attempt to explain this favouritism to me, a small child trying to understand why his needs often came first. "Remember," she said, "he's the favourite—until one of you is unwell." I wasn't sure what that meant then, but I felt the quiet tension beneath her words.

In 1996, our search for a new home brought us back to England. I was eager to return 'home' to family, but leaving behind the life I loved in Scotland was heart-wrenching. Our new house was found in a small Nottinghamshire village, and the moving date was set. April 1st, 1996—a day marked by my grandfather's 66th birthday and my brother's scheduled surgery—was to be our moving day. It seemed like everything that could go wrong had already gathered for this one, heavy day.

- **Dunblane**

Wednesday, 13th March 1996. A day etched in my soul forever. A man — a vile insult to the word *man* — whom I refuse to name because he does not deserve that recognition, stormed into Dunblane Primary School. Armed with four handguns and over 700 bullets, he ruthlessly stole the lives of sixteen beautiful, innocent children and their wonderful teacher. He wounded several others before ending his own life, leaving a community shattered beyond repair. It was a day that broke the world as I knew it — a day that changed everything. Lives were lost, hearts were shattered, and the innocent light of childhood was forever dimmed. It touched millions across the globe, sparking a change in UK gun laws, but for me, it was the moment everything I believed about safety and love was violently torn away.

I was eight years old, in Primary 4, sitting in that school on that terrifying day. I consider myself incredibly lucky — fortunate beyond words — to have escaped injury, to have my family spared from the direct horror. But still, that day fractured the innocent little girl I was, scattering pieces of me that would take years, decades even, to find and heal. The trauma settled deep inside me, invisible but suffocating.

The details of the day blur and twist in my mind, fragmented and disjointed — but some moments remain vivid, burned into my memory by fear and confusion.

My classmates and I, lined up quietly with our teacher, were walking down the corridor as we always did, heading toward the GP room. I think we were going to practice songs for an upcoming assembly — something lighthearted, familiar, ordinary. Then, without warning, the calm was shattered by the terrifying sound of sharp, relentless bangs echoing off the walls. Tiny holes suddenly appeared in the plaster, and jagged cracks splintered through the glass windows that looked out onto the cold, grey concrete playground. My best friend and I exchanged confused whispers, trying to make sense of it all. "It must be building work," we told each other, clinging to that fragile explanation, our innocent minds refusing to believe that something so normal could suddenly become so terrifyingly wrong.

Across the playground, I saw a figure standing in the fire exit doorway of the gym. I couldn't see a face, couldn't comprehend what this stranger was doing there. The thought never crossed my mind that this figure was shooting at us, trying to kill us all. I was a child — naive and trusting — and I believed I was safe.

Then, chaos unfolded. We were ordered to drop to our hands and knees, crawling frantically to a classroom where we huddled behind a teacher's desk, trembling and silent. How long we waited, I don't know. Five minutes? Thirty? Hours? Time lost all meaning in those moments. Later, we were moved to the GP room, packed among other terrified children, sitting in rows but learning nothing — just waiting, trapped in a nightmare without understanding.

No one told us the truth yet. The horror had not reached us fully. But I remember my best friend's tears, her anguished cries for her little sister. My own tears caught in my throat, my heart pounding, as I prayed silently for my brother — knowing somehow, deep inside, that he was safe. My friend's worst fears were true. Her beautiful baby sister was among those shot, stolen from this world forever. Sometimes I wonder if she cried because she *knew* too, even before the truth was spoken.

When our parents finally arrived, the names were called out like a cruel roll call. My mum's arms wrapped around me in a tight, fierce hug in what felt like the darkest corridor in the world. I don't remember the words spoken, only the overwhelming safety in that embrace — a fragile shield against the terrifying unknown.

At home, silence blanketed the house. Neighbours came by, tears streaming, holding us close. The television flickered with news reports, displaying the names and faces of those lost. A wave of sorrow so vast, so incomprehensible, washed over me. I was only eight, and yet my small mind tried desperately to grasp the magnitude of the tragedy unfolding around me.

I didn't fully understand then. But I *felt* it — the weight of the loss, the sudden, brutal emptiness where joy and innocence once lived. My world had shifted beneath my feet, and I was left unsteady, lost in fear.

The weeks that followed were a blur of grief and confusion. Friends came to play at the house, trying to piece together a shattered reality with shared stories and whispered fears. My mum watched silently, knowing we needed to face the trauma, even as it tore at her heart. Nightmares became my constant companion. I would wake screaming, convinced that everyone I loved had been taken from me. The dreams replayed the horror — part memory, part news footage — an unrelenting film that refused to be erased.

I became afraid of everything — the dark, shadows outside my window, strangers, the silence. I needed a light on every night, clinging to comfort until I was almost grown. I cried until someone came to hold me, to soothe the terror that gripped my little body. The fear stayed with me, a shadow trailing through my childhood and beyond.

Before we left Dunblane, I went to my best friend's house one last time. The silence there was heavy, the memories of her sister everywhere. I sat on the back of the sofa, singing Celine Dion's *Think Twice* — but we changed the words, "Baby" became "Amy." She begged me not to leave, and I cried, not wanting to abandon her when she needed me most. But I had no choice. Leaving her behind, knowing the pain she carried, planted a seed of guilt inside me — a seed that has grown and shaped the way I love and protect others to this day.

The town was swarmed by reporters for what felt like an eternity. We lost our privacy, our space to grieve. Cameras invaded our gardens and homes.

The nation watched our pain unfold, and we were unable to mourn in peace.

I never officially returned to Dunblane Primary School after that day. Just once, before we moved, I visited to gather my things. Walking through the corridors, boarded-up windows and all, I was met with quiet kindness from Mrs McTurk, my wonderful class teacher. My mum explained why we were there, and my best friend was excused from class to say goodbye. We cried, held each other tightly, standing in that same corridor where terror had struck so recently. The guilt of leaving her alone, of walking away from that shared trauma, weighs on me still — shaping the broken, fragile person I became.

Then we left — driving away from Dunblane, from what was once home, to start over in England. But I was no longer the same little girl. I was broken. And that break, that fracture of my childhood, would ripple through every part of my life to come.

- **The move to England**

Just nineteen days after the massacre, we left Scotland behind and moved to England. It should have been a fresh start—a new house in a quiet, idyllic village, nestled among green fields and winding country lanes. But my heart was still back there, shattered and buried beneath the weight of what I had lived through. Nothing felt new or fresh. Everything hurt. My soul was bruised, my innocence gone, and my sense of safety erased.

My parents had purchased a home they planned to renovate. The village had a primary school within walking distance, small and welcoming. My brother and I were enrolled almost immediately. He entered Year 6, and I started in Year 4.

I remember our first school assembly clearly. The entire student body was gathered in the hall. I sat amongst the rows of unfamiliar faces. The headteacher, Mr. Eveleigh, introduced us kindly, his voice calm and warm. I remember feeling his presence like a blanket—soft, reassuring. He was a good man. He noticed the fear behind my polite smiles and the anxiety in my fidgeting hands. Whenever I looked worried or withdrawn, he would check in, always with gentleness. He made me feel seen, even when I wished I could disappear.

One day, while I sat at my desk, working on something I can't even remember now, I glanced out of the window toward the playground. There it was—the little wooden picket fence that surrounded the yard. It was barely four feet tall. A person could climb it in seconds, or just walk through the unlocked gate. And suddenly, that familiar tidal wave of fear surged inside me. My breath caught in my throat. My hands trembled. Because in that moment, I realised: this school wasn't safe. No school was. Anyone could come. It could all happen again.

I broke down completely. I was hysterical, sobbing, shaking, inconsolable. My classmates stared. My teacher tried to calm me down. But nothing could penetrate the terror. To them, it probably looked like an overreaction—a child with an overactive imagination. But for me, it was real. It had happened before. And if it could happen once, why not again?

At night, sleep was no refuge. I had relentless, graphic nightmares. Every time I closed my eyes, I was back in that hallway, hearing the bangs, seeing the glass shatter, feeling the confusion and terror of that moment. I would wake up screaming, soaked in sweat, heart racing. My mum tried her best to comfort me, but I don't think anyone knew what to do. There wasn't a manual for parenting a traumatised child.

I was grieving—not just the event, not just the victims, but the person I was before. I no longer felt like a child. I felt like a fragile shell of someone who used to believe the world was kind. I was afraid of everything—loud noises, unfamiliar places, being left alone, the dark, people. Even things that used to bring me joy felt laced with danger. My nervous system was constantly in high alert, my shoulders always tense, my stomach always tight.

Despite this, I tried to find normalcy. Two girls lived just a few houses away, and I quickly clung to their friendship. I'd knock on their door almost every day, desperate for distraction, craving connection. When we played, I could sometimes forget. I'd smile, laugh even. I wanted to be a normal kid so badly. And for a few fleeting moments, I could pretend I was.

But the cracks were always there. My light had dimmed. I was more needy, more sensitive, more prone to withdrawing or bursting into tears over small things. Beneath the surface, I was still broken.

My mum, knowing I needed more than she could give, sought out therapy for me. I never made it past the first session. She initially attended alone to explain my background, only to find when she returned with me that the room was filled with students, eager to use me as a case study. When she asked if anyone there was qualified to help a child like me and got no answer, she walked out. We never went back. That was it—the one chance I had at healing was taken away before it even began. I wouldn't receive any mental health support until adulthood.

Back then, I didn't understand the magnitude of that loss. But looking back, I feel an overwhelming grief for the little girl I was—the one who kept asking for help in all the ways she knew how, and who was continually let down. I've often wondered who I might have become if I'd been properly supported. How might my story have changed?

Instead, I carried my trauma silently into adolescence. As I entered my pre-teen years, everything got harder. My emotions were volatile and intense, made worse by puberty and the lack of tools to process anything I was feeling. I didn't understand myself. I couldn't make sense of the way my moods swung violently, or why I felt like I was constantly on the verge of exploding or collapsing.

Home life became strained. My family and I clashed often. I was unpredictable, moody, easily overwhelmed. To them, I imagine I was exhausting—hard to live with, impossible to comfort. But I wasn't being difficult on purpose. I was lost. My sadness and fear had no outlet, so they spilled out in frustration, anger, and arguments over the smallest things.

I was punished more than I was consoled. Grounded, shouted at, criticised. I felt like a disappointment. Like a problem. Like I was fundamentally unlovable. My stepfather was distant, my brother intolerant, my mum overwhelmed. I don't think any of them understood what I was going through. I barely understood it myself. I was drowning in a sea of emotions with no one to throw me a life ring.

Despite all of this, I tried to live. I made friends at school and in the village. I was outgoing and sociable, always seeking connection. But underneath, I was desperate for acceptance and terrified of abandonment. I was always second-guessing whether people really liked me. Often, I didn't believe they did. I thought I was too much—too emotional, too intense, too broken.

Not everyone was kind. One day, a girl in the village named Hannah gathered a group of kids to surround me on their bikes. They started throwing devil bangers—those little paper fireworks that explode with a loud bang—around me. The sound was deafening. Each pop sent me spiralling back to that hallway in Dunblane. I froze, terrified, my heart pounding so loudly I could barely hear them laughing. It was cruel, and it broke me. After that, I avoided socialising with certain people in the village. I didn't feel safe with them either.

Thankfully, I also found true, lasting friendship. One girl—Sarah, though we all call her Molly—became a constant presence in my life. She's been by my side through every storm since then. Her loyalty, her kindness, her steady presence—she gave me something to hold on to when everything else felt like it was falling apart.

Still, no amount of friendship could undo the trauma. Every day felt like a battle to function. Secondary school was tough. I wore a mask of humour and bravado to hide my fear. I became the joker, the tough one, pretending I didn't care. But I did. I cared so much it hurt. I just didn't know how to show it. I lashed out at others, and sometimes, others lashed out at me. Once, a girl punched me, for no apparent reason. There were fallouts, cruel words, physical fights. I didn't know how to maintain stable relationships. I didn't know how to be okay.

Life at home didn't get easier. My emotional struggles continued to affect everyone around me. I was constantly in trouble, always being told I was the problem. I believed it. I internalised every word. I thought there was something wrong with me. That I was fundamentally flawed.

Now, as an adult, I see it differently. I wasn't bad. I wasn't broken. I was traumatised. I was crying out for help in the only ways I knew how. I needed support, not punishment. I needed compassion, not criticism.

I often wonder how different things might have been if someone—anyone—had truly seen me back then. If someone had stepped in and said, "You are not the problem. What happened to you was the problem."

Maybe I would have believed it. Maybe I would have healed sooner.

But I'm healing now. I'm finding my way back to that little girl—the one who was brave and kind and full of life before the world broke her. I'm learning to give her the love she never received. I'm learning to let her know: none of it was her fault.

PART 4 - GROWING UP EMOTIONALLY UNSTABLE

- **Life at Home**

I think now is a good time to talk about family life—and the impact I believe it had on my emotional instability. As with any story, there are always two sides, and this is mine. My truth, told through the lens of my lived experience. I'm sure my family members remember things differently. And that's okay. But what I *do* know is this: I was an incredibly sensitive child, especially after Dunblane. I wore my heart on my sleeve, and every feeling—big or small—landed in me like a storm.

I've said before, and I still believe it to be true—I was loved. My family loved me. But love doesn't always protect you from pain. Sometimes, it's tangled up in it. So often, I felt like the root of every problem. The one who caused the tension, the drama, the upset. I adored my mum. To me, she was the best, most supportive mother anyone could hope for. But it's only since becoming a parent myself that I've begun to see things through a different lens. The rose-tinted view I clung to for so long has faded, and I'm now able to recognise the quieter, more insidious patterns—narcissistic traits, emotional manipulation, and the slow erosion of my sense of self. All the things that made me feel, at my core, unwanted. Not enough.

My brother, on the other hand, seemed to move through life without carrying the same weight. The trauma of Dunblane didn't seem to settle in him the way it did in me. He thrived—at school, in sports, socially. He had a steady calmness about him, like the world just made sense. He was good at everything. He was easy. And me? I was the opposite. Loud. Emotional. Lost. Always searching for a place to belong—even in my own home.

Relationships at home were often strained. After we moved back to England, my mum and stepdad split up. I remember lying awake at night, listening to their angry voices leaking through the walls. I even remember the day it became official—being picked up from the local youth club and taken to Leicester, to my grandparents' house. I wasn't heartbroken. I actually told my mum, "Well, at least we don't have to deal with that grumpy bastard anymore."

But time, as it does, softened things. And eventually, my mum chose to give the marriage another go. My stepdad moved back in, and it was as if none of it had ever happened. The tension returned, wrapped in the disguise of normality.

My relationship with my stepdad was always strained, no matter how hard I tried to fix it. And oh, how I tried. I craved a father figure in the home, someone warm, someone who made me feel safe. I was a loving child—full of hugs and hopeful gestures. But he was the opposite. Miserable. Cold. Awkward. It felt like he resented joy itself. Simple things turned into battles. I wasn't allowed to sing in the car. He hoarded food, then let it rot. He said "no" as a default, until my mum eventually persuaded him otherwise.

He wasn't physically abusive—I understand that. But his cruelty came in other forms. He was emotionally distant and rigid. He seemed to enjoy making life harder than it needed to be. I wanted to love him. I wanted *him* to love *me*. But he never did—not in any way I could feel. And growing up in that atmosphere, where warmth was rationed and kindness felt conditional, left invisible bruises I carried for years.

He made it clear I irritated him. He mocked me under the guise of humour, calling it "just a joke" when his words stung. He had a habit of giving people cruel, sometimes racist, nicknames. His comments weren't offhand—they were sharp, deliberate. He *knew* where to aim. And as someone already raw with sensitivity, it hurt more than I can describe. What

I needed most was gentleness. What I got was contempt dressed up as sarcasm.

His presence was a constant reminder that I didn't quite belong. That I was too much, too loud, too emotional, too *me*. Over time, that message became louder—with every jab, every eye-roll, every look of irritation, every private joke that wasn't really funny. The older I got, the deeper that wound became.

Despite it all, I clung to my relationship with my mum like a life raft. To me, she was everything—my best friend, my anchor, my safe place. I leaned on her for everything. It was as though I never really stepped into adulthood, because I still needed her opinion on every little thing. All I ever wanted was to make her proud, to feel like I was enough in her eyes. And maybe I was, sometimes. But there was always this subtle undertone—a quiet but persistent sense that I was falling short. That I'd never quite measure up to my brother.

He was everything I wasn't. Smart, confident, accomplished. He carried himself with ease, while I stumbled through emotions that felt too big for my body. I was full of fire and fragility, loud laughter and quiet tears. I struggled to believe in myself. I always felt like I was bothering people just by existing. If it wasn't my stepdad sighing in frustration, it was my brother's disapproval. If not him, it was my mum's disappointment, or a comment from my grandparents. There was always someone reminding me I was too much, or not enough—rarely just right.

Every criticism chipped away at my self-worth. Every "why can't you just…" carved out a piece of my identity. I didn't recognise it then—I just absorbed it, like a sponge. I believed it. I *was* the problem. I *had* to be better. If I could just get it right, maybe they'd finally love me the way I needed them to.

I can admit now—I wasn't easy. I was intense. Sensitive. Exhausting, maybe. But I wasn't bad. Still, I was made to feel like I was. I'll never forget the day my mum told me my brother had sat her down and asked, "When are you going to give up on her?" Like I was some failed project. Something broken. Something disposable.

I did act out in my teens. I rebelled. I drank, smoked, fell too fast for people who couldn't love me back. Not because I wanted to be difficult—but because I was *desperate*. Desperate to feel loved. Seen. Safe. I wasn't a nightmare—I was a girl in pain.

Through therapy and deep reflection, I've finally begun to understand myself. I now see how the constant criticism, the emotional coldness, and the feeling of being the family punchline shaped how I saw the world—and myself. Emotional instability often comes with a deep fear of being abandoned, of being unworthy of love. And maybe that fear was always a part of me. But I also believe it was fertilised by the environment I grew up in—where love was conditional, approval was rare, and being "too much" meant being cast out.

Sometimes I wonder if my emotional struggles were born from the trauma of Dunblane. But more and more, I think they were forged in the quiet heartbreaks of childhood—in the loneliness, the rejection, the endless trying to be enough.

- **Teenage Trauma**

The arrival of teenage hormones was like pouring petrol on a fire that was already burning out of control. I was already drowning in emotions I didn't understand, and now they came at me with the force of a tidal wave—

sudden, overwhelming, and completely unpredictable. Life became a relentless rollercoaster, with mood swings so violent they left me reeling. One moment I'd be euphoric, laughing with friends, and the next I'd be spiralling into despair, convinced I was broken beyond repair. The highs were frantic and fleeting; the lows felt endless. It was emotional whiplash—and I never knew when the next drop was coming.

My insecurities grew louder, more demanding, like a voice in my head I couldn't silence. I didn't know who I was, let alone where I fit in the world. I felt like I was floating outside of myself, watching everyone else get it right while I stumbled through a fog of self-doubt and invisible pain. Home offered no comfort. It felt heavy, stifling—a place where I was constantly reminded of all the ways I didn't measure up. So, I stayed away as much as I could.

Being with friends gave me space to breathe. Surrounded by noise, laughter, and distraction, I could quiet the intrusive thoughts and mute the ache that followed me everywhere. I wasn't trying to be reckless—I was just trying to feel *okay*. To feel *something* that didn't hurt.

Like most teens, we got into mischief—drinking cheap cider in the park, sneaking cigarettes behind the bus shelter, and causing low-level chaos we thought made us cool: teepeeing trees, tagging the bus shelter with bad graffiti, exploring old buildings that smelled like damp and danger. We weren't hardened troublemakers—we were just kids, aching for excitement and escape, desperate to feel like we belonged *somewhere*. I look back now and smile at some of it, even cringe a little—but I also see a girl who was just trying to cope the only way she knew how. And as a mum now, I get it. I really do. My God, I'd be mortified if my own kids were doing the same.

I know the teenage years are turbulent for most—a messy blur of self-discovery, emotional highs and lows, and inevitable clashes with family. But for me, it went deeper than that. It wasn't just angst or moodiness—it was a gnawing, relentless emptiness. A crushing sense of not being enough, of being somehow defective at my very core. The lack of self-worth I carried wasn't just a passing phase—it was a constant, heavy ache in my chest that coloured everything.

I was starved for love, for validation, for someone—*anyone*—to see me, to want me, to tell me I mattered. I wasn't looking for drama or attention for the sake of it—I was trying to fill a void that felt bottomless. I would morph into whatever I thought people wanted me to be, just to belong. Just to feel safe. I needed to be in a relationship—not because I was in love, but because the idea of being alone felt unbearable. Being wanted, even temporarily, helped quiet the inner voice that told me I was worthless. It made me feel like I had a place, even if that place was fragile or fleeting.

In 2001, at the tender age of 14, deep into those chaotic years of teenage rebellion, I found myself hooked up with an old primary school friend. Our groups of friends all gathered at one of their houses, drinking, laughing, and searching for a kind of freedom we didn't really understand yet. I remember how we kept slipping away together, sneaking off to the bathroom for stolen kisses and shy touches. Every second of his attention felt like a balm on a wound I had carried for years—a desperate, aching hole inside me that longed to be filled. I clung to those moments, believing that his interest meant I was finally seen, finally wanted.

We were both incredibly drunk when we left that night, and he offered to walk me home. I remember the cold air by the river that ran through our village, the quiet darkness wrapping around us as we lay down together, fooling around, two kids caught between innocence and something more. In that moment, I thought I wanted what he wanted—I wanted to feel close, to be loved. But when he started trying to have sex with me, the pain was overwhelming. It was like my body was betraying me, like I was being torn open from the inside, raw and unprepared. I told him to stop, that it hurt too much, but he didn't listen. For what felt like an eternity, he kept pushing, ignoring the only voice that mattered—mine.

Inside, panic erupted like a storm. I was trapped in a body that refused to protect me, too drunk, too weak to push him away. I couldn't escape. Time blurred, and I was left with only the sound of my own terrified heartbeat pounding in my ears. Eventually, he stopped. We got up, and he walked me home in silence—like nothing had happened.

The next day, I tried to reach out, to find some acknowledgment, some sign that he cared. But he looked through me like I was nothing—like I was some dirty little secret to be discarded. The shame I felt crushed me. I was more broken than ever—unwanted, unlovable, and stained in ways words can't fully capture. I knew he should have stopped when I said it hurt too much. But I also knew I had said yes before I said no, and so I buried the blame deep inside myself. I was the one who had failed, I told myself. I was the one who had lost control.

After that night, I lost pieces of myself I never found again. My confidence shattered into dust, and I became even more desperate—more hollow—yearning for someone, anyone, to love me enough to never hurt me like that again.

I carried that unbearable pain with me for months, each day growing heavier, until finally, on December 1st, 2001—my brother's 17th birthday—I reached a breaking point I couldn't undo. It began with yet another argument with my mum, this time because she'd found out I'd sworn in art class at school. It felt like just another drop in the endless flood of clashes between us, a routine neither of us seemed able to escape. But that day, the fight spiralled faster than usual. In a moment I still struggle to process, she pinned me to a chair by my throat. I screamed for her to get off me, my voice cracking with terror, begging her not to hurt me. That was the first—and only—time my mum showed violence, but the fear it ignited in me burned deeply and hasn't faded.

Afterward, I was sent to my room, left alone with the echo of what had just happened. My hands trembled as I found a bottle of prescription painkillers—meant for my period pains—that sat quietly on my bedside table. I remember sinking into a place so dark and vast, overwhelmed by a crushing loneliness and a sadness that swallowed me whole. I felt like nothing more than an annoyance, a burden that everyone around me would be better off without. The silence around me was suffocating, and I believed, with every aching fibre of my being, that the world would be better off without me in it. I counted out the tablets, one by one, swallowing them numbly, my vision blurring as the room tilted and spun. Twelve pills went down, and as I reached for the thirteenth, something invisible—something fierce—stopped my hand. I couldn't bring it to my mouth. To this day, I believe someone was watching over me that night—a guardian angel, or maybe my great-grandad, Grandpa Fowkes, silently protecting me from beyond, refusing to let me take that last step.

Not long after, my mum's voice called down the stairs, snapping through the fog of numbness. She told me to walk the dog and help prepare birthday tea for my brother. I said nothing about what I'd done, barely able to speak, and quietly agreed. I moved like a ghost, drifting through a haze that separated me from the world, from reality. Somehow, I managed the walk and returned home, but inside, I was nothing but empty and lost, in a complete daze.

Back in the kitchen, Mum asked me to make the vol-au-vents for dinner. As I took a step forward, my legs betrayed me, collapsing beneath my weight. I remember Mum's frantic efforts to get me to the living room sofa, but then darkness swallowed me whole. Mum later told me I'd had seizures, and an ambulance was called to rush me to Lincoln Hospital. On the way, paramedics warned her to prepare for the worst—that I was unlikely to survive the overdose. I didn't know then how perilously close I'd come to death, but looking back, I see how fragile my life had become. The medication I'd taken had two possible endings: death or recovery. Somehow, I was lucky enough to be the latter.

My memories of hospital are fragmented, a hazy blur of consciousness and seizures. I remember I woke once and asked my mum a simple, childish question: why all the doctors seemed so grumpy. She told me they were frustrated, burdened with caring for people who were truly sick, and that I was wasting their time. Their coldness landed like a blow to my chest—it was as if my pain was invisible, unworthy of care or concern.

When I was finally fully conscious, Mum questioned me about what had happened. While I'd been unconscious, I had spoken about my sexual experience, naming the boy involved. I later learned Mum went to his house after leaving the hospital, though I don't know what exactly she said to his parents. From that day forward, I felt the crushing weight of their hatred—his family, his friends, and him made it clear I was unwanted. That rejection tore open the raw wound inside me again, bleeding deeper than before. I felt utterly alone—not just in that moment, but for years afterward—like a broken thing everyone wanted to forget, discarded and invisible, carrying scars that no one saw.

- **The Aftermath**

After my suicide attempt, much of my time slipped away in the sterile, quiet halls of the hospital—trapped alone with my racing, dark thoughts. Visits from my mum were rare and vague in my memory, her presence more a shadow than a comfort. My dad showed up once or twice, but even those moments felt like distant echoes from a world I couldn't reach. I was caught in an invisible bubble, a space where no one truly saw or understood the storm raging inside me. When I was finally allowed home, the walls closed in tighter still. Mum immediately grounded me—no contact with friends, no support, just a suffocating silence that swallowed me whole. I don't even know if my friends knew what had happened.

She made me take a pregnancy test, then took me to get screened for STIs. Thankfully, everything came back clear, but the whole ordeal felt less like care and more like punishment—a reminder that I had somehow broken the fragile balance of our family. At no point did anyone ask how I was really doing—no gentle check-ins, no offers of therapy or real support. The world around me stayed cold and indifferent. I was still the family's black sheep, blamed for every problem, carrying the weight of unspoken disappointment and anger. Inside, I was utterly alone, a burden I felt everyone wished would just disappear. The silence around my pain was deafening, like a wall closing in tighter with every breath I took.

As the months dragged on, I searched desperately everywhere outside myself for love and acceptance—any flicker of warmth to hold on to. I reached out to friends and their families, to kind elderly neighbours who welcomed me in, anyone who might patch the emptiness gnawing at my soul. But with that search came a crushing wave of shame. Any boy who showed me even the smallest spark of interest became my whole world. I gave everything—physically, sexually—in a misguided attempt to prove my worth, to make myself feel seen and wanted. I let myself be used, reduced to nothing more than an object to satisfy others, as long as they offered even a flicker of affection.

The void inside me was ravenous, swallowing every bit of self-respect I had left. I pushed my own needs, my own feelings, to the back of my mind, sacrificing myself in a desperate bid to keep those fleeting connections alive. Whether it was because of the fractured, cold world I lived in at home, a trauma response, or something buried deeper inside me, the loneliness was unbearable. The ache for belonging and love was so raw, so desperate, that I was willing to lose myself entirely in anyone who showed even the faintest glimpse of care.

- **Sexual abuse**

In my desperate search for love, I unknowingly opened the door to a dark world of sexual abuse. I became an easy target for predators—so vulnerable and starved for affection that they didn't even have to try. With just a twinkle in their eye, I would fall at their feet, offering myself without hesitation, With so little self-worth, no confidence, and no real sense of who I was, I was drawn straight into the arms of my 27-year-old bus driver when I was just 15. Most of what happened between us has been buried deep in my memory—a trauma response that kept those moments locked away until very recently, when fragments began to resurface. But I do remember the way he talked to me—flirting with a casual confidence, calling me 'Tiger' with a big cheesy grin and a wink. In that moment, I was completely hooked. The idea that a grown man could actually be interested in *me* felt almost unreal, like I'd finally been seen and wanted in a way I'd never known before. I don't remember exactly how we exchanged numbers, but soon we were texting and talking every day. At the time, I believed we were building a relationship—something real and mutual. Looking back now, I see clearly that it wasn't a relationship at all. It was grooming, manipulation, and sexual abuse by a fully grown man, taking advantage of my vulnerability and desperate need for affection.

What has probably hit me the hardest since realizing I was sexually abused is that my mum allowed it to happen. I vividly remember this man coming to our house, and my mum having a private conversation with him downstairs before letting him come upstairs to hang out with me. I don't know what they said during that conversation, but somehow, the relationship was permitted to continue. He was given free access to me by the one person who should have been my protector—and that betrayal still cuts deeply. I was even allowed to go on trips with him in his car — we travelled to Skegness together and later visited my cousin who lived in Leicestershire. On the journey back, we stopped in a layby, where we began to have sex. That moment marked a painful turning point for me. I remember my feelings shifting in that moment — the overwhelming infatuation I'd felt vanished instantly, replaced by a cold numbness. I knew deep down it was wrong, and my mind just shut down, shutting him out completely. I didn't want anything to do with him anymore. I don't recall ever speaking to him again after that, and I certainly never spoke about what happened — not to anyone, ever. It wasn't until a few months ago, during a Child Sexual Abuse training event, that the long-buried memory resurfaced, forcing me to confront a past I had tried so hard to forget.

My experiences of being sexually abused continued from the age of 15-17, when my brother's friend, who was a regular visitor to our house, began to come to my bedroom at night 'to say goodnight' but would kiss me, rub himself against me and get me to touch him and perform sex acts on him. I don't know what my parents or brother thought he was doing, but no one ever questioned or challenged him about coming up to my bedroom. Weeks turned into months, and the abuse continued unchecked until it finally stopped when he left the village to go to university—by then, I was 17 and he was 18.

However, once again, I never stopped it. I now understand that, in some twisted way, it was meeting my unmet needs. In those moments when he came to see me and gave me attention, I felt wanted — I wasn't alone anymore. Someone was interested in me, maybe even cared. When it was just the two of us, he was so kind, and I truly believed he liked me. I knew he had a girlfriend, but he still came to see me. I never asked him to, but in my mind, that made me just as guilty because I didn't stop him. I gave him everything he wanted, desperate for even the smallest flicker of affection, even though I knew he was in a long-term relationship. I never spoke up. Back then, I thought it was my fault.

Now, I recognise that I was still a child — vulnerable, confused, and trapped in a cycle of abuse and trauma that was never processed and has weighed on me my entire life. Understanding this has helped me reflect on the person I became in early adulthood. It's allowed me to accept those broken parts of myself that led me to treat myself and others so poorly, and, in some way, begin to forgive myself.

- **The big wide world of adulthood**

Turning 18 felt like stepping into a world of possibility—a doorway to freedom that I had longed for, yet it came wrapped in the fragile skin of a deeply wounded, fractured young woman. I held in my hands a driver's license, a car key, a passport—symbols of adulthood and independence. On paper, I was free to roam anywhere, to shape my own future. I had a steady job, a small income, and still lived at home, where rent was just a fraction of what others paid. Friends surrounded me, and I was constantly out—dinners that buzzed with laughter, late nights in crowded clubs, festivals where music drowned out the noise in my head, and holidays that promised escape. I even managed to build a career that, to outsiders, looked like success.

But beneath the surface, I was unravelling.

My emotions roared inside me like a storm without pause. Every feeling was magnified—pain was unbearable, anger volcanic, joy overwhelming—and I had no filter to protect me from the intensity. The smallest things could shatter me: a dress that didn't feel right, a careless word from a friend, a simple misunderstanding. These tiny cracks would widen until I was left sobbing or raging alone in my room. I chased numbness and distraction in reckless ways—partying until dawn, drowning my fears in alcohol, chasing highs with drugs, smoking like it was the only steady rhythm. I gave my body away to men who looked through me, never seeing the brokenness I tried to hide, never caring for more than a moment's pleasure. I didn't care about myself either. Why would I?

Inside, I was a tempest of rage, despair, desperation, and self-hatred. I clung fiercely to any flicker of affection, afraid of being invisible, desperate not to be abandoned. My temper flared easily, scaring away the very people I wanted to keep close. Beneath the chaos and glittering nights was a soul quietly crumbling—a soul screaming for someone, anyone, to see the drowning girl beneath the surface.

At home, the tension had eased just enough to create a fragile peace. I learned to quiet my voice, swallowing the defiance that once burned so brightly. My brother had moved out and was building a life far from the turbulence that defined my days. My maternal grandparents had moved nearby, their presence like a double-edged sword—offering stability but also heavy expectations. They watched closely, shaping me with their own ideas of who I should be, how I should behave, how I should carry myself. Their love came tethered to rules and judgments, leaving me feeling more like a project to fix than a person to be understood. And so, I danced a careful dance between craving connection and retreating into the safety of silence.

- **My First True Love**

The day before my 20th birthday, I was sitting in my friend's car in the local McDonald's car park when Ryan and his best mate pulled up beside us. We'd all gone to school together, but Ryan and I had never really spoken before. That day, something shifted. We ended up catching up over a McDonald's meal and a smoke in the nearby woods. From the moment we started talking, there was an instant connection—a quiet, effortless comfort I'd never experienced before.

We exchanged numbers, and I invited them both out for my birthday the next night. That evening, Ryan and I laughed, flirted, and peeled back the layers of each other's lives. He was different—genuinely kind, soft-spoken, respectful, and warm. His presence was calm and steady, a stark contrast to the chaos I was used to. He didn't take from me or demand anything; he simply showed up with sincerity and care.

For the first time, I glimpsed what real love could be—what it felt like to be treated with gentleness and dignity. Yet, beneath it all, I was still broken. I loved him more deeply than I had anyone else, but I didn't fully understand just how rare and irreplaceable he was. Looking back, I see the preciousness of that love—the healing it might have brought—if only I'd been ready to accept it.

Ryan carried his own heavy burden. He had lost his older brother to suicide nearly four years before we met. Though he rarely spoke of it, I saw the weight of that grief in his eyes. It was a silent pain that never left him, and it broke my heart knowing I couldn't lift it from his shoulders.

We shared an intense 11-month relationship, falling deeply in love, moving into a small, terraced house together, and continuing the party lifestyle—but now, as a couple.

But trauma and alcohol are a volatile mix. I was still emotionally shattered from years of unprocessed abuse and chaos, and I was probably at my most fragile then. Ryan, on the other hand, had shut down completely, unable to process his own pain. We both carried too much hurt, and cracks soon appeared. Our drinking often escalated into explosive fights that left us gasping with regret. Eventually, we drifted apart.

Heartbroken doesn't even begin to cover what I felt when he left. When we split, it felt like my whole world shattered. I cried harder over losing Ryan than I ever had over anything else. I had believed he was my future—the one I'd marry, have children with, grow old beside. And suddenly, he was gone. Just like that. No pleading, no tears could bring him back. Not yet, anyway.

I moved back home and sank into the darkest depression I'd ever known. I stopped caring if I lived or died. I refused to wear a seatbelt when I drove. I stopped eating properly. I drank more, used more drugs, and slept with more men—each encounter a desperate attempt to fill the gaping hole Ryan left behind. I hated myself, truly. I spiralled into a pit of self-loathing so deep I became an easy target for anyone wanting to exploit vulnerability. I met men who used me, lied to me, stole from me, and treated me like I was worth nothing.

And still, I didn't stop. I kept chasing love like it was the very air I needed to breathe—desperate to feel wanted, desperate for someone to see in me what I couldn't see in myself. Desperate to be loved, because I had never learned how to love myself.

PART 5 - AN EMOTIONALLY UNSTABLE MARRIAGE

- **Head Over Heels**

In April 2010, at just 22 years old, I bought my first home — a milestone that should have filled me with pride and hope. It was a dream made possible by an incredibly generous gift from my maternal Grandad, and on paper, it marked the beginning of a new chapter. A fresh start. A foundation to build something beautiful on.

And that's when I met *him*. The man I would eventually marry.

From the very beginning, he swept me off my feet with an intensity that felt like destiny. He showed up during one of the darkest seasons of my life — when I was still quietly bleeding from old wounds I hadn't even acknowledged. Somehow, he knew the exact words to say. Words that wrapped around me like bandages. Words that felt like healing, like hope, like maybe — just maybe — I wasn't too broken to be loved.

His love didn't whisper; it roared. It felt like oxygen in a world where I'd spent too long gasping for breath. And I fell — hard. Fast. Completely.

We became inseparable almost immediately, as though we were each other's missing piece. Every waking hour was spent together. He was attentive, passionate, and overflowing with affection. What might have looked like a whirlwind romance to others felt like salvation to me. I clung to him like he was the only thing keeping me afloat.

But somewhere inside that all-consuming love, I began to disappear.

Piece by piece, my sense of self began to erode. I stopped seeing my friends. I let go of my routines, my ambitions, my independence — all the things that made me *me*. I gave up anything that didn't revolve around him.

I was trying to be what he needed, trying to hold onto the only kind of love I'd ever believed I was worthy of — one that demanded everything in return.

We would spend countless nights curled up indoors, eating takeaways and watching films, trying to fill the emptiness we both carried. But the hunger wasn't physical. I was starving for validation, desperate for someone to *stay*. And he did. That felt like enough to ignore the way my mental health was quietly crumbling beneath the surface.

As my body changed — gaining weight rapidly, retreating from the world — so too did my mind. My anxiety became constant, a background hum that turned into a deafening roar. Depression wrapped itself around me like a heavy blanket I couldn't shake. I became afraid to leave the house. Panic attacks struck like lightning. I was haunted by memories I didn't yet know how to face. But even then, I didn't seek help. I didn't want to ruin what I thought was the only good thing I had. He was *still there*. And to me, that meant more than anything.

When my friends reached out, worried by my silence, I brushed it off. I'd disappeared from their lives, yes — but only because I was finally *happy*, wasn't I? When I did mention their concerns, he told me they were jealous, manipulative, only pretending to care. He convinced me that they didn't want to see me loved — they wanted me broken, the old me, the fun one who partied and laughed and self-destructed for their entertainment. Slowly, his words replaced my reality. His voice became the only one I trusted.

And so, my friendships dissolved, not with a bang but a long, aching silence. Not because they stopped trying — they *begged* me to see what was happening. But I had already made my choice. I chose him. Over everything and everyone. Even Molly, who had stood by me through it all had to give up trying eventually and take a step back, with us not speaking at all for many, many months. I missed her getting married and so many key moments in her life. It wasn't until many years later, when I was beginning to recognise the toxicity and narcissism of my husband that I approached her again, apologising profusely for turning my back, for being so cold and for not seeing the truths they were trying to make me aware of.

My health continued to spiral. I was signed off work for almost six months. I was drowning in fatigue, both physical and emotional. I was diagnosed with fibromyalgia, anxiety, and depression. It felt like my body and mind were screaming for help, and yet all I could focus on was keeping him happy. I truly believed that if I could just *love him enough*, everything would be okay.

Even as my mum voiced her concerns — gently, but with increasing desperation — I couldn't hear her. She saw what I couldn't: the way he was slowly taking over my life. He barely worked, just a few hours a week delivering pizzas, yet he was living with me, sharing my space, my food, my finances. I was slipping into debt just trying to make our little bubble feel like a home. She watched as I changed — in body, in spirit, in every possible way — and she tried to pull me back. But I was already too far gone.

Looking back now, with years of distance and heartache between then and now, I can finally see what I couldn't at the time: I wasn't in love. I was drowning in co-dependency. I had mistaken intensity for intimacy, control for care. I didn't fall in love with a person — I fell into a desperate need to feel chosen, to feel worthy, to feel *enough*.

But in giving everything to him, I lost the one thing I needed most —
myself.

- **The first big bust up**

Not long into the relationship, my mum and grandparents made a reasonable request. If he was going to live with me — in the home I'd just bought, with a deposit gifted entirely by my Grandad — then he should sign something. A simple agreement. One that stated he had no claim to the property if we ever separated.

At the time, I completely understood. My family weren't being cruel. They were protecting me — their daughter, their granddaughter — trying to make sure I kept the security they had worked so hard to give me. It was fair. Logical. Sensible.

So, I brought it up. Gently. I told him my mum would draw something up. I thought if I explained it with care, if I led with reassurance, he'd understand too.

But instead, he exploded.

I will never forget the sheer violence of that reaction. His face twisted in outrage, his voice like thunder. He said I was accusing him of being a gold-digger. That I obviously didn't trust him. That if I truly loved him, I'd never even consider something so insulting. It wasn't just anger — it was betrayal. He made me feel like I had stabbed him in the heart.

And I panicked. I crumbled. I spiralled.

I followed him down the stairs, sobbing, clawing at the air as if I could hold onto him with my desperation. My shame was so thick I could barely breathe. The terror of losing him was so loud in my ears that I couldn't think straight. I started pulling at my hair, scratching at my skin, completely lost in that frantic, feral state I knew all too well — where emotional pain became physical, where punishment felt like the only way to survive.

Then I grabbed a knife.

I didn't think. I didn't plan. I just needed the noise in my head to stop. Needed the feeling of control, of something real cutting through the panic. I began sawing at my arm. Not just a cry for help — this was something else. Something deeper. Something darker.

He found me like that. Came rushing in. Pulled me back. Wrestled the knife from my hand. And when I collapsed to the floor, gasping, screaming, drowning in a panic attack so intense I thought I'd die — he didn't leave.

He stayed. He calmed me. Soothed me.

And that small act — staying — cemented something devastating in my mind: *He must love me. He didn't abandon me. He saved me.* And in my trauma-shaped brain, that meant I owed him everything.

But eventually, he *did* leave. Said he needed space. Needed to think. That maybe he couldn't be with someone who was so unstable. So broken.

I believed him. Every word. I *was* broken. I *was* too much. And still, I ached for him to come back.

A few days passed. When he returned, something in him had changed. He was cold. Calculated. There was no warmth left in his voice when he said, "That was not okay. You're not normal. But I'll stay… if you drop the contract."

I felt torn in half. Betraying my family was unthinkable — after everything they had given me. But the idea of losing him again was unbearable. I had already decided that I couldn't live without him. That this love — toxic, consuming, all-encompassing — was my only tether to life.

So, I dropped the contract.

And with that one decision, the power shifted entirely. From then on, I would spend years trying to prove I was worthy of being loved. Years trying to atone for a crime I never committed.

When I told my family, the fallout was immediate — and brutal. My mum and stepdad came over to "talk it through." It was a disaster. You see, when two narcissists fight for control over the same person, the result is a war zone. They didn't come to listen. They came to win.

My stepdad nearly came to blows with my partner. The atmosphere was suffocating. Aggressive. I sat between them, silent, splintering into pieces. I couldn't defend either side. I couldn't tell my mum that I felt she was overstepping. I couldn't tell him that he was being paranoid and cruel. I was stuck. Trapped in the middle. The rope in a vicious tug of war between the two people I needed most.

After that night, I was cut off. My mum and I barely spoke for months. And even when we did eventually reconnect, the damage was done. The trust was gone. The bond we'd built over decades shattered like glass beneath my feet.

And I let her down her all over again when I bought a new house with him - again, with no contract, no protection. I gave him everything. Let him live in a home funded almost entirely by my family's generosity, without any claim of fairness or balance. I just wanted peace. I wanted to believe in love.

But love should never require the loss of everyone else in your life. It should never cost your voice, your freedom, your safety.

He refused to have anything to do with my family for the rest of our 7 year relationship. My mum never felt comfortable in our home. My extended family disappeared from my life. And when things inevitably turned bad — as they often did — I had no one. Nowhere to go. No one to call. He had slowly, methodically, made sure I was alone.

He told me over and over that my friends didn't really care. That my family just wanted to control me. That *he* was the only one who truly loved me — the only one who saw me.

I remember one fight where my mum screamed, "Tell him he's fucking won!"

And I screamed back, "It's not a game! This is my *life*! I'm not a prize to be won!"

But the truth is, by then, I didn't even feel like a person. I was just a shadow of who I used to be.

Raised in an emotionally abusive household, starving for affection and approval, I had become the perfect target. I was fragile. Malleable. Eager to please. And he took full advantage.

I didn't *love* my husband in the traditional sense. I *worshipped* him. I surrendered to him. My only purpose became keeping him happy — no matter the cost to myself.

But loving a narcissist is like trying to fill a bottomless well. No matter how much you give, it is never enough.

I remember sobbing in front of him, asking why he was so cruel. Why he said such awful things to me.

He looked at me — deadpan — and said, "I know I'm doing it. But I can't stop myself."

And somehow, I stayed. Because I thought if I just loved him enough, I could fix him. That if I tried harder, he'd stop hurting me. But that moment marked the beginning of a darker descent.

My self-harm escalated. My breakdowns became more frequent. I began slamming my head into walls, clawing at my face, anything to release the internal torment. I was lost inside myself, drowning in a sea of pain I didn't know how to name.

Then my sex drive disappeared. Completely.

Maybe it was the antidepressants. Maybe it was trauma. Or maybe — it was my body finally rejecting the emotional abuse it had endured for so long. Either way, it was gone.

He was furious.

He made me feel defective. Unlovable. He punished me with silence, with coldness. Withholding affection unless I gave him sex. He told me no other man would tolerate my "crazy" — especially if I wasn't even willing to satisfy them.

So I gave in. Out of guilt. Obligation. Pity. Every week, at most every 2 weeks, I would have to betray myself and my own needs and give him what he wanted.

It became a duty, not a choice. A performance, not a connection.

And then... it got worse.

He started masturbating beside me while I slept. Then touching me in my sleep. *Inside me.* His favourite thing was to rub his fingers around and inside my body while I lay unconscious.

I lost count of how many times I woke up in a daze, confused, violated — and yet, convinced it was normal. He made it sound so casual. So reasonable. He needed release. I was his partner. This was just how things were.

I didn't know it then, but I was being raped.

And perhaps the most painful part of it all? I believed so deeply I *deserved it*.

- **The Awakening**

Life continued like this for years — a relentless loop of highs and lows, each one more exhausting than the last. I lived in cycles of chaos, of tension and brief relief, clinging to moments of peace like they were proof I wasn't crazy. But the truth was always the same: no matter how toxic things became, the blame always landed on me.

According to him, my mental health was the root of all our problems.

And I believed him.

I genuinely thought I was the issue. That I was too difficult to love, too emotionally unstable to live with. And honestly, I wasn't easy to be around — I was reactive, self-destructive, often lost inside my own storms. But looking back now, I can't help but wonder...

Had I been treated with love, with patience and respect — would I have ever gotten that bad?

Who knows.

In a desperate attempt to feel better — to feel anything other than broken — I started searching for answers elsewhere. I stumbled across the world of spirituality. The Law of Attraction. The idea that we create our own reality with our thoughts and energy.

It felt like hope.

So, I threw myself into it. Books. YouTube videos. Podcasts. I spent hours soaking in every new concept, every whisper of truth that said: *You are powerful. You have choice.*

For the first time, I saw a crack in the wall that had trapped me for so long.

The more I learned, the stronger I became. The more I practiced gratitude, the more I could feel glimpses of something new — peace. I started focusing on what felt good, even if it was just the smell of coffee in the morning or the softness of my dog's ears. I stopped giving so much weight to other people's moods, other people's opinions.

I realised I could choose how I responded. That I didn't have to internalise every outburst, every insult. I didn't have to hand over my power just to keep someone else calm.

It was a quiet rebellion — but it was mine.

This new way of thinking sparked something in me. A flicker of light. The first glimmers of *self-love*. I began to picture a different kind of life. One where I wasn't constantly walking on eggshells. One where I didn't live in fear of saying the wrong thing. A life where I could be appreciated, not criticised. Loved, not controlled.

But the brighter I got… the darker things became at home.

My growth seemed to provoke him. The more I smiled, the more he sneered. The more peace I found within myself, the more he tried to drag me back down. Like he could feel his grip slipping — and he didn't like it.

And when I stumbled — which of course, I did — he was right there, waiting.

The second I dipped back into anxiety or sadness, the second I made a mistake or reacted emotionally, it was like he hit *play* on a well-rehearsed script.

"This is your fault. You're the problem. You always have been."

And deep down, I still believed it.

Somewhere in the confusion, I didn't just *accept* that narrative — I *became* it. I wore it like a second skin. I made it my identity: the unstable one. The damaged one. The one who should be grateful anyone stuck around.

So, when he asked me to marry him, of course I said yes.

It was Christmas. The ring was my present — or at least, that's how he framed it. But I paid for it myself. That detail barely registered at the time. I was too busy basking in the one thing I'd been chasing my whole life: someone *choosing* me.

I was over the moon.

For a moment, the pain didn't matter. The control, the manipulation, the years of emotional whiplash — none of it mattered, because here was a man who wanted to marry me. Who said he couldn't live without me. Who claimed to love me so much, he couldn't bear the thought of losing me.

He was possessive, yes. But to my trauma-wired heart, that felt like passion. Obsession felt like devotion. And devotion felt like safety.

I didn't yet know that obsession isn't love. That control isn't protection. That dependency isn't intimacy.

But I would learn. The hard way.

- **The Wedding**

The wedding — what should have been the most joyful day of my life, a celebration of love and commitment — instead became another quiet tragedy. Another fracture in a long line of breaks between me and the people who raised me.

By that point, things with my maternal family had just started to heal. Slowly. Cautiously. After years of silence and strain, there were signs of life again. My mum and I were speaking daily — brief chats, casual updates, tentative exchanges that tiptoed around the pain we hadn't yet dared to name. I had begun seeing my brother again. My grandparents, too. It wasn't perfect, and the undercurrent of hurt still hummed in the background, but for the first time in years, there was something that almost resembled a family. Something fragile and hopeful. Something I could nearly believe in.

And then, the wedding — another test. Another ultimatum. Another choice.

He told me he didn't want a big wedding.

That part I understood. The thought of being the centre of attention made my skin crawl. I hated being watched, hated the pressure of smiling just right, saying the right thing, looking the part. A small ceremony suited me. I agreed.

But then he said, *"I don't want your family there."*

Not my mum or Dad. Not my grandparents. Not my brother. Not anyone.

He wrapped it up in silk: "It'll just be a peaceful, intimate moment," he said. "Just you, me, and a couple of close friends. No drama. No judgement. No stress."

But I knew what it really was. Another line drawn in the sand. Another layer of isolation. Another way of making me prove my loyalty.

And so, I did what I'd always done — I chose him.

I swallowed the lump in my throat and told myself this was love. That sacrifices were part of commitment. That maybe, just maybe, my family would understand — or at least forgive me in time.

But deep down, I knew they wouldn't.

We got married in the local registry office. Two of our friends were witnesses. His mum sat quietly at the side. I wore a dress I'd bought cheaply online, simple and elegant. My hair was styled, my makeup carefully applied. I looked like a bride. I smiled like a bride. I posed for photos like a bride.

But I didn't *feel* like a bride.

There was no one walking me down the aisle. No one waiting with tears of joy in their eyes. No speeches. No laughter. No shared glances from proud parents or clinking glasses or soft embraces.

Just a sterile room. A man who claimed to love me. A silence so thick it was suffocating.

I texted my mum. Sent her photos. Me in my dress. Me with my make-up and hair beautifully done. Me smiling with eyes that didn't sparkle the way I'd hoped they would. I waited for something — a message, a word, a heart emoji. Anything.

But nothing came.

She said nothing.

And in that silence, I felt like I disappeared.

That night, after we'd gone home and climbed into bed — still in my makeup, hair beginning to fall loose around my face — I lay there beside the man I'd married and sobbed quietly into my pillow. Not from joy. Not from the emotional high of a long-awaited day.

But from grief.

A deep, heavy grief that pressed against my chest and made it hard to breathe.

I had done everything I could to protect peace, to avoid confrontation, to follow love wherever it led me — even when it led me straight into loneliness. I had tiptoed around everyone's expectations, tried to make space for every version of "right," and still, no one seemed happy. Not my family. Not my husband.

Not even me.

I had married the man I thought I couldn't live without. I had convinced myself that once we were husband and wife, things would finally settle. That I would feel safe. Anchored. *Chosen.*

But lying there in the dark, his back turned to me, my wedding ring still tight on my finger — I had never felt more alone.

There was no sense of celebration. No glow. Just a woman in a white dress, crying herself to sleep beside a man who had made sure she walked into her future with no one by her side but him.

And still, I called it love.

Because I didn't know what else to call the ache I was willing to live with, just to avoid being left behind.

- **Unfaithful Motherfucker**

Married life was no better.
In fact, it was worse.
So much worse.

There was no honeymoon phase. No fresh start. No new promises blooming in the soft glow of commitment. Just the same toxicity — now cemented with vows and legal binding. Just the same cold silences, sharp criticisms, and relentless gaslighting, now wrapped in the illusion of permanence.

The ink had barely dried on the marriage certificate, and already I felt it — that deep, sinking sense of *I've made a mistake*. But it was more than that. It was a sense of *now I'm trapped*.

He hadn't changed.

If anything, he became more emboldened. More entitled. He had me now. I had said *yes*. I had chosen him. So, what right did I have to protest? To withdraw? To have boundaries?

My world had shrunk entirely to fit inside his. There was nothing else. No one else. Just him.

Most days, the only sliver of freedom I felt came during work — a few fleeting hours where I could breathe without anticipating his next mood swing. Where I wasn't being dissected by his glares or punished with silence. Work became the only space where I still felt like a person. Not just a burden. Not just someone failing to be enough.

And then, came *the betrayal*.

He didn't even have the decency to hide it well. Or to be ashamed.

Apparently, the perceived lack of sex in our marriage — something he never missed a chance to remind me about — had finally become unbearable for him. So instead of talking to me, instead of working through it with compassion or care, he did what cowards do: he found someone else to stroke his ego.

A girl from his past. Someone he hadn't spoken to in years. He messaged her. Reached out. Poured his heart out — not in honest vulnerability, but in that manipulative, self-pitying way he'd perfected. He painted himself as the victim. A man suffering in a cold, sexless marriage with a broken, unstable wife. And of course, the conversation turned sexual.

He confessed it to me like he was being noble. Like telling the truth somehow earned him back moral high ground.

He told me — like it was nothing — that she had said I sounded boring.
Boring.
That word landed like a slap. Because I wasn't just *hurt* — I was humiliated. Reduced.

But that wasn't even the worst of it.

He admitted to sending her *a photo*. Not just any photo. Not just some shirtless selfie or flirty snap.
A photo of *us*.
Together.
In the middle of something intimate. Something I had allowed — trusted — shared in a rare moment when I let my guard down.

And he sent it to another woman.

His justification?

"Don't worry. I put an emoji over your face."

Like that made it okay. Like that made it less of a violation.

My entire body went cold. I remember my hands shaking. My stomach flipping. A kind of slow, nauseating disbelief flooding every inch of me. I couldn't speak. I couldn't cry. I just sat there — stunned — as the last illusion I had about him crumbled.

I had always believed — or *wanted* to believe — that despite everything, he would *never* cheat. That the control, the possessiveness, the emotional abuse… was twisted love. Messy love. But love nonetheless. I thought he was broken. Damaged. But loyal.

That illusion died that day.

He didn't love me.
He loved power.
He loved control.
He loved knowing that no matter what he did, I would *stay*.

And of course, he made it about me.
He reminded me — again — of how unhappy he was. How he had *told* me he needed more sex. That he had *warned* me. That this was just the natural consequence of my failure to meet his needs.

And like always, I absorbed it.

So completely. So effortlessly.

I told myself it was my fault.
I was broken.
I was emotionally unstable.
I was the reason he needed someone else.

I remember it so clearly: just an hour after he dropped this emotional bomb on me, I had a doctor's appointment. I sat in that waiting room, heart racing, trying to breathe like a normal person. I smiled politely at the receptionist. Answered questions. Let them weigh me. Check my blood pressure. As if I wasn't completely hollowed out inside.

When I got home, still dazed, he was already over it.

He said, "If we're going to move forward, you need to forgive me. Now. You can't bring it up again. If you do, it means you're not letting it go. And *that* means *you're* the one stopping us from healing."

So, I swallowed it.
Because that's what I did.
Over and over again.

I buried my pain deep down into that familiar well — the one already overflowing with all the other betrayals I'd never been allowed to name.

I smiled.

I carried on.

I told myself this was marriage. This was what people did. They worked through things. They sacrificed.

But deep down, I knew.

I was still clinging to a version of love that didn't exist.

And I was married to a man who had betrayed me in one of the most intimate, violating ways imaginable — and then had the audacity to blame *me* for it.

And still…

Somewhere in the wreckage,

I believed I was the problem.

- **Another Unsuccessful Attempt**

A few weeks later, another explosive argument erupted between us.

I can't even remember what it was about now — that's how frequent and predictable they'd become.

Just background noise in our everyday chaos. One long, looping cycle of conflict, rage, and despair.

But this one was different.

This time, he actually walked out.

No dramatic exit.

No yelling over his shoulder.

No promise to come back and "talk things through."

He just… left.

For all the volcanic fights we'd had over the years — the screaming, the swearing, the venom — he had never physically left me in the middle of it.

Not once.

No matter how toxic things got, he stayed.

He hovered.

He loomed.
And even in that, there was a twisted kind of predictability.
But not this time.
This time, the house was silent.

And the silence he left behind was deafening.

I broke.
Completely.

It felt like something inside me — something vital — just split in two. I couldn't breathe. Couldn't think.

My whole body pulsed with panic. My brain was a battleground of cruel, looping thoughts, each one louder and sharper than the last:

You're worthless.
You're broken.
You're unlovable.
You ruin everything.
This is always going to be your life.

I couldn't escape them.
They were everywhere.
Inside my skull. Under my skin. In the air around me.
I clawed at my arms just to *feel* something different — anything other than the anguish. But even that old, familiar coping mechanism didn't work this time.

It wasn't enough.

Nothing was enough.

I needed it to stop.
All of it.
The pain. The noise. The shame. The relentless ache of trying to be loved by someone who only ever made me feel invisible.

I went to the garage.

I didn't even think.
I just *moved*.

I found an old skipping rope, tied it into a makeshift noose, and hooked it onto one of the exposed beams. The whole thing felt mechanical. Hollow. Like watching someone else go through the motions.

I dragged over his weights bench, climbed up. My knees shook. My whole body trembled. Tears poured down my face, but I couldn't even feel them.

I looped the rope around my neck.

And I just stood there —

Teetering.

Paralysed.
One step.
That's all it would take.
Just one step, and I'd be free.

No more trying.
No more performing.
No more walking on eggshells.

No more explaining my pain to someone who refused to see it.
No more begging to be enough.

Just… peace.

And then —

I heard the garage door creak.

The sound jolted through me like lightning.
He had come home.

My heart stopped.
My breath caught.
I was frozen — caught in the act. Caught at my lowest, most desperate moment.
Terror. Relief. Shame. Exposure. They all hit me at once, crashing down like waves in a storm.

He walked in.
He saw me.
Standing on a bench.
A rope around my neck.
Shaking. Crying. Barely holding on.

And you know what he said?

"You stupid bitch. What the hell are you trying to do to me?"

No rush to hold me.
No panic.
No grabbing the rope.
No, *"Are you okay?"*

No, *"Please, don't do this."*

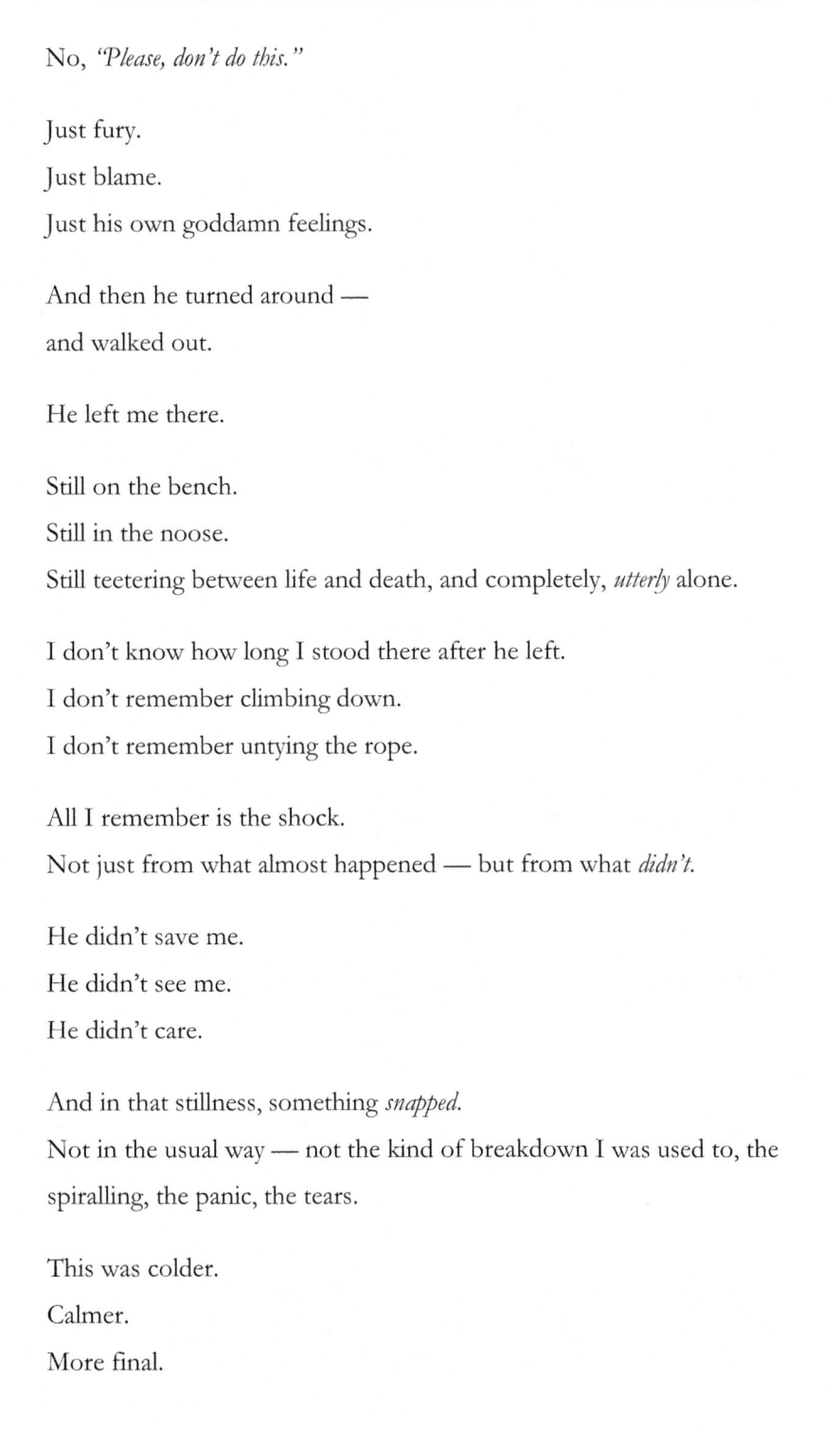

Just fury.

Just blame.

Just his own goddamn feelings.

And then he turned around —

and walked out.

He left me there.

Still on the bench.

Still in the noose.

Still teetering between life and death, and completely, *utterly* alone.

I don't know how long I stood there after he left.

I don't remember climbing down.

I don't remember untying the rope.

All I remember is the shock.

Not just from what almost happened — but from what *didn't*.

He didn't save me.

He didn't see me.

He didn't care.

And in that stillness, something *snapped*.

Not in the usual way — not the kind of breakdown I was used to, the spiralling, the panic, the tears.

This was colder.

Calmer.

More final.

It was like my heart put up a wall to protect itself, and for the first time, I saw him.

Truly saw him.

I saw the emotional parasite I had married.
The man who had spent years draining me, silencing me, gaslighting me, controlling me.
The man who could walk into a room, find his wife seconds away from dying, and still make it about *himself*.

And I saw *myself*, too.
Or rather, who I had become:
A woman who no longer recognised her own reflection.
A woman who had spent so long begging to be loved, she forgot she was already worthy of it.
A woman who was surviving, barely, in a marriage that was quietly killing her.

In that moment, I knew.
This was not love.
This was not okay.
This was not survivable.

Something in me went quiet.
Cold.
Detached.
I shut down emotionally.

Whatever string had kept me clinging to the hope that he would change, that we could be happy, that *I* could somehow fix this — it snapped clean.

And though I stayed — physically — for a while longer, emotionally, I left that day.

That was the moment I began the process of *unloving* him.
Of mourning the fantasy.
Of slowly crawling back to myself, from the darkest place I had ever been.

- **Therapy, Therapy, Therapy**

After the incident in the garage, something inside me shifted — not a lightning bolt of clarity, not some grand revelation, but a quiet, stubborn voice whispering, *You cannot survive another round of this.* It wasn't dramatic. It wasn't even hopeful. It was just… necessary. I couldn't keep pretending I was okay. The mask had slipped — violently, publicly, fatally close — and I didn't have the energy to put it back on.

So, I did the unthinkable, for me. I asked for help.

I sat in the GP's office, numb but shaking, barely holding myself together. I remember the fluorescent lights above me flickering slightly, the stiff fabric of the chair beneath me, the way my fingers trembled as I spoke. And for the first time in a long time — maybe ever — I told the truth. Not all of it, but enough to show the cracks. Enough to say: *I'm not okay. I don't want to be here anymore.*

That admission, so small and so enormous, opened a door. I was referred to the crisis team, and suddenly I had access to something I had only ever dreamed of — therapeutic support. Actual people, trained to help people like me. People who didn't know me, who didn't carry years of judgment or fatigue or resentment. Just therapists. Strangers. Safe ones.

I started a course of CBT — Cognitive Behavioural Therapy — the first structured attempt to untangle the chaos in my head. I turned up to every session, polite and attentive, doing the homework, practising the techniques. I *wanted* it to work. God, I *needed* it to work. I was so desperate to feel human again — or at least functional. But the truth? CBT didn't even scratch the surface.

The therapist gave me tools: how to challenge my thoughts, how to reframe them, how to spot the patterns. But when your brain is a battlefield, none of that matters. When your nervous system is constantly in survival mode, logic doesn't stand a chance. I'd leave sessions feeling like I'd failed. I couldn't think my way out of a tidal wave.

During those early sessions, I also underwent some assessments. Routine things, apparently. But it was there, in that clinical, impersonal process, that someone flagged my emotional instability for the very first time. A passing comment. A note in a file. Not a diagnosis. Not even a conversation. Just an invisible label I wouldn't learn existed until nearly a decade later, when I accessed my own medical records. *Emotionally Unstable traits.* That's what they called it.

Back then, I had no idea that what I was living with might be more than trauma or sadness or "just a bad temper." I thought I was simply a broken person with a malfunctioning personality. I had no idea that my intensity, my fear of abandonment, my spirals and my swings — all of it — had a name. A reason. I just thought I was *too much*. Unfixable. Fucked up.

But I kept searching. I wasn't ready to give up.

When CBT didn't help, I reached for something else — something softer, more intuitive. A hypnotist, a friend of my mum's, offered to help. I grabbed the opportunity like a lifeline. We met regularly. She was kind, gentle, soothing. Her voice would guide me into trance states, help me visualise calmer futures, remind my body it could feel safe again. I'd lie there, still and open, letting the weight of her words settle into my bones like medicine.

And for a while, it helped — not dramatically, but enough to survive. Enough to function. She didn't ask too many hard questions. I didn't offer too many hard truths.

Because I wasn't being honest. Not fully. Not even close.

I didn't tell her about the rope. About the garage. About the moment I stood inches from death. I didn't talk about how shattered I still felt after my husband's betrayal, or the shame that soaked every part of me like a second skin. I didn't say, *I'm scared of him. I don't trust myself. I feel like a burden simply for existing.* I talked about surface things: my stress, my anger, my mood swings. The parts that were socially acceptable. Easier to digest.

Inside, though, the war raged on.

There were days I felt a little lighter. Days I could make a meal, smile at a stranger, even laugh without it catching in my throat. But none of it felt solid. I was still so fragile — like one wrong word, one cold glance, one slammed door could shatter me all over again.

I was surviving. Barely. Not living — not yet.

But somewhere deep down, there was still a tiny, flickering light. A belief that maybe — *maybe* — life wasn't supposed to feel this way. That maybe the world wasn't meant to be a minefield. That maybe love wasn't supposed to hurt so much.

So, I kept reaching.

Every self-help book I could get my hands on. Every YouTube video on healing, manifestation, energy, the Law of Attraction. I clung to these things like a starving person clings to crumbs. I watched others talk about joy, about freedom, about creating the life you dream of — and something in me believed them. Or at least, *wanted* to.

Because I knew, in my bones, this wasn't it.

This wasn't what my life was meant to be. Not this cage of shame and survival. Not this exhaustion. Not this aching loneliness, even in the presence of someone who claimed to love me.

And I didn't have a plan. I had no map. No solid support system. No diagnosis to explain why I felt like I was constantly drowning in my own emotions.

But I knew, with a clarity that terrified me:
If I didn't find a way out — not just from him, but from the storm inside me — I wasn't going to make it to thirty.

PART 6 - AN EMOTIONALLY UNSTABLE ENDING

- The Medium

One day, a friend and I decided to book in with a local medium. We'd heard glowing reviews — people saying she was the real deal, that her readings brought peace, closure, even clarity. I didn't know what I believed. Part of me thought it was probably bullshit — wishful thinking dressed up as spiritual guidance. But another part of me, a deeper part, was desperate. Desperate for something to make sense. For something to tell me that I wasn't alone in all of this chaos. That maybe the pain I was carrying had a purpose, or at the very least, a witness.

I didn't go looking for answers that day. I went looking for hope — or maybe just a moment of stillness in the storm. My world had been spinning for so long, chaos clinging to every corner of my life, that I think I would have done anything for a pause button. Just one moment where something — anything — made sense. Part of me needed to believe that there was more to this life than just surviving it. More than the pain, the loneliness, the relentless ache that had carved itself into my chest. I needed to believe that I was being held by something bigger than all of this — that I wasn't just drifting through the wreckage on my own.

I prayed — not in a structured or religious way, but from that desperate place inside your soul that doesn't know what else to do. I whispered into the void, hoping that maybe someone was listening. That maybe my beautiful Nana — the one person whose love had ever felt truly unconditional — was still close somehow. Still watching. Still guiding. I begged the universe, quietly and without ceremony, to give me a sign that she hadn't really left me. That she could see how hard I was trying to keep going. That she might somehow be leading me toward something softer, something safer. A better existence. A life that didn't hurt so much.

I didn't know what I was hoping to find in that reading. Maybe peace. Maybe proof. Or maybe just permission to believe that I hadn't been forgotten by the people — and the parts of myself — that I loved the most.

My friend went in first while I waited in a quiet side room. I remember the way my heart thudded in my chest, not from fear, but from this strange anticipation. Like I was standing at the edge of something I couldn't name yet. When it was finally my turn, I stepped into the softly lit room and sat down at the table across from the medium. She was calm, warm, unassuming. Not theatrical like I'd expected. Just present. Grounded. I tried to quiet the noise in my head as the reading began.

It started the way I expected — vague but pleasant. Generic comments about energy, some mentions of past hurt and future growth. Nothing bad, but nothing deeply resonant either. I was already preparing myself to smile politely and chalk it up to another box ticked in my weird healing journey.

But then something shifted.

Her tone changed — sharpened, more focused. She grew more insistent, asking me if I knew someone who had passed in a sudden, tragic way. She described the death as a suicide. Someone young. Male. She asked if that meant anything to me. I shook my head, confused. Over and over again, I said no. I didn't know anyone like that. At least, not *personally*. Not *directly*.

But she wouldn't let it go.

She repeated the message, growing more certain. "He's saying he's with his dad," she said. "He's okay. They're both okay." And then something about a brother. A brother sending love. A brother needing to hear this.

And then — like a lightning bolt — it hit me.

Ryan.

I hadn't seen or spoken to Ryan in years. We'd both gone our separate ways, married other people, built lives that no longer touched. But once, he had been everything to me. My first real love. The first person who made me feel safe in my own skin. The first boy who saw me — really saw me — when I didn't even know who I was yet.

And his brother had taken his own life.

I felt the air leave my lungs. The room went still.

I told her. I told the medium who Ryan was — that we weren't in contact, that we had history but no current connection. That it would be strange, even inappropriate, to just reach out after all this time with something so personal, so intense. But she didn't flinch. She looked at me steadily, like she knew something I didn't. And then she said, plainly, "You'll be in touch. It's already decided."

Those words sat heavy in my chest as I left. I didn't know whether to laugh or cry. I was torn between thinking it was all a coincidence and feeling — *knowing* — on some primal level, that it wasn't. That this wasn't random. That somehow, across all this time and distance, something was trying to bring us back into alignment. Not for romance. Not for drama. But for something... unresolved.

I couldn't stop thinking about him.

The message haunted me. Not just in the way it lingered, but in the way it *unsettled* something buried deep inside me. In the quiet moments — lying in bed at night, sitting alone at a red light, staring blankly at a wall — I kept picturing him. Wondering how he was. Wondering if he still remembered me, if he would even care to hear this message, or if it would just reopen an old wound best left closed.

Eventually, curiosity gave way to something stronger. *Responsibility*. I searched him on Facebook — not to message, just to look. Just to see if the medium had been right.

And there it was.

His dad had passed away.

The grief on his timeline was raw. Real. I stared at the screen, a lump forming in my throat. I hadn't known. I hadn't been there. And yet, somehow, the message had still found its way to me.

Suddenly, it didn't feel like an option anymore. I had to pass it on. Whether he believed it or not, whether it mattered or not — it had to be said.

I messaged his ex-sister-in-law — someone I'd always got on with and I knew was still involved with the family. I told her everything. What the medium had said. How strange it all felt. I asked if, when the moment was right, she could maybe share it with Ryan. No pressure. No expectation. Just a whisper of kindness passed along.

To my surprise, she replied quickly and warmly. She thanked me. Told me he'd had a really rough year — his marriage had ended, and he was now raising his children on his own. My heart cracked open. Not out of pity. Not even out of guilt. But because even after all these years, after all we'd both been through, I still cared.

And maybe that was the most painful part. Realising that the love I thought I'd buried under years of trauma, disappointment, and survival… had never really gone away.

She passed the message on to him. A while later, I heard back that Ryan had thanked me. That was it. No follow-up. No flood of emotion. Just a quiet acknowledgement. But in that simplicity, I felt something shift. Like I'd completed a loop. Like a piece of my past — one of the only pieces that had ever felt truly safe — had finally come full circle.

But something else had awakened, too.

A soft ache. A long-forgotten hum in my chest. Not longing in the romantic sense — not yet — but something deeper. A recognition. A remembering. A tiny voice whispering, *There's something here.* Not just with him, but within *me*. Something I'd buried when life got too loud, too painful, too chaotic. A part of me that remembered what it felt like to be loved gently. To be seen.

That night, I lay in bed thinking about all the versions of myself I'd been. The broken girl who begged to be enough. The woman who was surviving a marriage that almost killed her spirit. The fighter. The seeker.

And the girl who once loved Ryan with a pure, quiet kind of love that had no idea how complicated life would become.

And somehow, I knew — I wasn't done with that story yet.

- **Making Contact**

A few weeks after the reading, I cracked.

I'd tried to hold the line, telling myself it was just a strange coincidence, a fluke, a glitch in the universe that didn't mean anything. But the truth was, it haunted me. That message — his brother, his dad, the insistence that it was for *me* — echoed in my mind like a song I couldn't turn off. I wasn't trying to rekindle old flames or stir up old wounds. I was just trying to *breathe*. Trying to honour something that had found its way to me with such undeniable force.

Still, I fought it. For days. Maybe weeks. I told myself to leave it alone. That I had enough mess in my life without inviting more complication. But the pull was magnetic. Unexplainable. So, with trembling fingers and a heart pounding against my ribs, I opened Facebook. Found Ryan's profile. Typed out a message. Deleted it. Typed it again.

It was simple. Careful. I apologised for reaching out to him out of the blue. Told him I'd heard he'd been having a hard time lately and that I was truly sorry. I hoped he was okay — like *really* okay. I didn't mention the medium, not yet. I didn't even know how to say any of that without sounding unhinged. I just wanted to offer something gentle. Human. A kindness, after so much silence.

And then — *ping*. A reply. Quicker than I'd expected.

He thanked me. Said the message I'd passed on — through his ex-sister-in-law — had meant something to him. That it had come at a strange and needed time. He asked how I was doing. Nothing fancy. No flood of emotion. But the simplicity of it — the *ease* of it — nearly undid me. After all that time, we were speaking again. Like no time had passed, but also like a thousand lifetimes *had*.

We reconnected on Facebook. Shared a few polite, familiar exchanges. It was nothing dramatic. Just soft threads of reconnection. But under the surface, something inside me stirred. Something that had been dormant for years. Like a frozen part of my heart had started to thaw.

Meanwhile, back at home, everything was collapsing.

My marriage had become unbearable. A cold, empty shell that echoed with arguments, silence, and unmet needs. I felt nothing when I looked at my husband anymore — not anger, not love, not even grief. Just numbness. Like watching a movie of someone else's life. We'd been circling around the topic of separation for months, years even, but neither of us could summon the courage to speak the words that would make it real. Fear kept us in the dance — fear of change, of pain, of what might happen if we let go completely.

But inside, I was already gone.

I had no one outside of him. No family safety net. No close friendships left. I'd become so enmeshed in his world that carving out my own felt not just daunting — it felt impossible. I was terrified. And yet, I knew I couldn't stay. Not and survive. Not and *live*.

And still — in the quiet spaces between the chaos — I thought about Ryan.

Then one day, I saw an update: Ryan had moved into a new home with his kids. On impulse, I sent a quick message. "Hope the move went well. Wishing you all the best in your new place." That was it. Innocent. Kind.

He replied. And again, the conversation flowed. Effortlessly.

But this time, it was different.

This time, there was truth.

I told him I hadn't stopped thinking about him since the medium reading. That something had stirred in me — a memory, a feeling, a knowing — and I couldn't shake it. That even after everything, some part of me still remembered what it was like to feel *safe*. To feel seen. Wanted. Loved. The words felt fragile as I typed them, like glass that might shatter under the weight of being too honest.

But he didn't run.

He said he felt the same. That he had been thinking about me too. That the message, the reconnection — it had meant more than he could explain.

And just like that, something shifted in me. It was like being cracked open from the inside out. Not in a destructive way — in a healing way. In a *remembering* way. As though I was finally touching a part of myself I thought had died a long time ago.

We started talking every day. About everything. His kids. Our struggles. Our past. Who we were now, and who we used to be. There was no pressure. No declarations. Just two people remembering how to be real with each other. In that space — raw, honest, open — I found clarity I hadn't had in years.

I had to leave.

Not for Ryan. Not for a fantasy. But for *me*. For the version of me I'd abandoned — the girl who had always longed for more than survival. I realised I'd been choosing pain because it was familiar. Because it felt like punishment. But I didn't want to live like that anymore. I deserved to choose peace. I deserved to choose myself.

But it was December. Christmas was looming. And even in my clarity, I couldn't bring myself to blow everything up just yet. As broken as things were, I still had compassion. I didn't want to blindside my husband, or ruin the holidays for anyone. I didn't want to add cruelty to the already crumbling mess. So, I made a silent vow to myself:

Get through Christmas. Play the part one last time. Keep the peace. And come January — leap.

Leap into the unknown. Into the fear. Into the truth.

Into the possibility of who I might become if I finally stopped abandoning myself.

Still, no matter what came next, one truth had settled deep into my bones — undeniable, quiet, and steady:

Ryan and I… we weren't finished.

Our story wasn't over.

Not even close.

– New Year, New Me?

New Year's Eve arrived like it always did — quietly, uneventfully. We had nothing planned, which wasn't unusual. Celebrating anything had become obsolete in our relationship. Birthdays, anniversaries, holidays… they passed us by in silence, swallowed by apathy. The idea of marking new beginnings felt almost laughable when we'd been stuck in the same loop for years.

That afternoon, my phone rang.

It was my stepsister — the one person who had remained a constant in my life, even as everything else unravelled. She had been there through my darkest moments — through depression, anxiety, self-destruction — always showing up, always holding space. So, when I heard her voice, sobbing, broken, I knew something was wrong. My stomach dropped before she even said the words.

Her boyfriend — someone I had never fully trusted, and definitely didn't like — had cheated. And this time, the cracks couldn't be plastered over. She was wrecked. I listened as she unravelled, her pain pouring through the phone line like static. I tried to soothe her, but my words felt empty. I could feel her sinking. And I couldn't let her spend the night alone, counting down into a new year that already felt tainted.

So, I offered to go to her. To stay the night. We'd see in the new year together — just the two of us. Not healed, not whole, but held.

I told my husband.

Asked if he minded — of course, he did.

Asked if he wanted to come — of course, he didn't.

I explained how upset she was. That she needed me. That this wasn't a party or an escape, but something necessary. He didn't care. He sulked. Threw emotional daggers disguised as offhand comments. Made it clear I was selfish. That I was choosing her over him — even though he had no intention of acknowledging the evening in any meaningful way.

I stood my ground. Told him, gently but firmly, that I was going anyway.

The air turned glacial. We barely spoke. His disapproval clung to me like smoke, but I was past caring. For once, I was doing what felt right. What felt kind. What felt *true*.

I drove to my sister's house with a strange cocktail of emotions — guilt, sadness, but also clarity. Something had shifted. As she cried and tried to make sense of her own heartbreak, I sat beside her, silently holding the shattered pieces of *my* life too. Only now, I was beginning to realise that I didn't want to glue them back together the same way. I didn't want to rebuild the old structure. I wanted to build *something else*.

At some point that night, I messaged Ryan.

We had been speaking almost daily by then, our connection deepening in quiet, unspoken ways. We still hadn't crossed any lines. Still hadn't named what this was. But the bond between us — it was real. It was undeniable.

That night, I told him the truth. I said I couldn't keep living the life I was in. That I didn't know exactly how or when, but I was going to leave. That I *had* to. I told him I hoped we could reconnect properly when the time was right — when I was free, whole, and ready to meet him honestly.

He didn't hesitate.

He said he wanted the same. That he'd been hoping, waiting, but never expecting. And with that one small exchange — so simple, so human — something in me crystallised.

The next morning, I drove home.

Back to the house that held all our unhappiness like a stale scent in the walls. I walked through the front door, into the quiet weight of resentment and denial — and I ended it.

Just like that.

I told him I was done. Not in anger. Not in theatrics. Just truth. I asked him to move out. And to my shock, he did. Without argument. Without fight. Maybe he was tired too. Maybe part of him had been waiting for me to say the words he couldn't.

And in that moment, I exhaled. Fully. For the first time in years.

I wish I could say we handled the aftermath with maturity. That we parted ways gracefully, untangled our lives respectfully. But that would be a lie.

Within weeks, the mask slipped.

He showed me who he really was — or maybe just who he had always been. He tried to lay claim on my home. And in the divorce proceedings demanded the exact amount of money my grandfather had gifted me — long before we'd even met. The money my family had *begged* me to protect from him.

And here he was, trying to take it anyway.

I was stunned. Not because he was being cruel — I'd seen that side before — but because a part of me still believed that at least *some* of it had been real. That he hadn't *just* used me. That the love — or whatever it was — had meant something.

But it hadn't. Not really. And now, there was no more pretending.

That was the final nail in the coffin.

I told him: do not contact me again. Ever. And from that moment on, he ceased to exist to me.

Dead. Gone. Irrelevant.

I have not spoken a single word to him since.

PART 7 - EMOTIONALLY UNSTABLE TRUE LOVE

- **Dreams Do Come True**

I have always considered the day my marriage ended as the day Ryan and I truly came together — not just as a couple, but as a family. Alongside his two wonderful children, Taylor and Laycie, we formed a bond that was immediate and unbreakable. From that moment on, we were utterly inseparable.

In the early days, when Ryan didn't have the kids, we spent long stretches of time together — days, nights, just us. Eventually, he introduced me to Taylor and Laycie, and I fell in love with them instantly. They were, and still are, the most amazing, adorable kids you could ever wish to know.

I remember our very first family day out — a trip to Mablethorpe Beach. We played in the sand, laughed in the arcades, and devoured fish and chips followed with melting ice-cream cones in hand. That day still stands as one of our favourite memories and places. From the moment I met them, Laycie became my little best friend. We've done, and continue to do, everything together. Taylor was a bit more reserved at first, taking his time to get to know and trust me, but now there's no one I'm closer to.

Being a stepparent has been the greatest blessing of all. What a beautiful gift it is to raise children you've chosen to share your life with — to be loved by them, not because you gave birth to them, but because you've become family by choice. It was everything I had always dreamed of, and more.

For a while, I felt stable. I was so happy that it felt like nothing could bring me down. I remember one conversation with Ryan, where I told him about my struggles with mental health over the years — how close I had come to ending my life just over a year before we met. I'll never forget what he said to me: *"Beautiful things happen when you don't give up."* And he was so, so right.

Because, while life has never been perfect, it has been truly beautiful since I met these three incredible humans — and even more so since we added our fourth, our little Hallie Rose, a beautiful baby of our own.

If someone had told me, back when I stood in the garage with a noose around my neck, that less than two years later I'd be living this life, I would never have believed it possible. From the edge of despair to an absolute dream — that has been my journey.

But it hasn't been all sunshine and rainbows. Over the years, we've faced some incredibly turbulent times. There have been battles with my mental health, family issues, health problems, and countless other life challenges that I'll share throughout this book. There were moments when we thought the storms might break us — as a couple and as individuals — moments when we felt we might not be strong enough to endure.

Yet here we stand today, stronger than ever. Ready to walk hand in hand through the rest of this journey called life.

If there's one thing I want you to take from this, it's this: no matter where you are right now, no matter how dark or impossible it feels, beautiful things *do* happen. Life *does* change. Happiness *is* waiting for you in the future.

So please — please don't ever give up.

- **Rebuilding Relationships**

My maternal family were relieved when I finally left my ex-husband, and over time, we rebuilt a stronger relationship. I'd maintained some level of contact with my mum for a while, but it had always been strained and difficult—largely because my husband completely refused to have anything to do with her. Even when I graduated from university in 2016, I had to choose whether I wanted my mum there or my husband, as he refused to attend if she was present.

In the months leading up to leaving my husband, I confided in my mum about the toxic behaviours I had tolerated for years—the mind games, control, and isolation. She was the one who encouraged me to look up the word *narcissist*, as she felt my ex perfectly fit the description. She was absolutely right. Suddenly, everything made sense. I realised that while my mental health struggles had played a part in the turbulence of our relationship and the extremes we faced, *I* was not the problem. The way he had treated me was absolutely not okay. Gradually, I came to understand that I had been in an abusive relationship—and my disgust toward him only grew.

My mum and the family supported me wholeheartedly through the separation, even paying for my divorce and financial settlement and clearing the debts I'd accumulated during the marriage. I felt truly welcomed back into the family, now that I had accepted I was in the wrong after all and that they had been right about him from the start.

But with that welcome came a heavy price. I questioned my own judgement so much that I couldn't make a single decision without consulting my mum. I became completely dependent on my family in every way possible. Throughout this time, I was repeatedly reminded that I had been the one in the wrong for trusting my husband—that I had been "the arsehole." It almost became a joke how much I was blamed for my past mistakes. I was reminded of things from my childhood and teenage years when I had supposedly "done wrong." I was once again the butt of the jokes, barely tolerated by my stepdad and feeling the resentment from my brother. I was back to being controlled and compliant to the family's expectations and demands.

And yet, I was convinced it was all love. I pushed down how those things made me feel. I ignored the voice inside me telling me something wasn't right—that it wasn't normal for a family to say such unkind things, to make me feel worthless, to refuse me the space to have different views or opinions. I remained certain that the problem was me—that I was the cause of all the family's problems.

Desperate for love and acceptance, I did everything I could to make things right. I ran errands, cleaned, dog-sat, house-sat, and helped my grandparents with anything I could. I became exactly who they expected me to be. I didn't voice my own opinions around my grandparents. I accepted that I had always been "difficult" and "hard work," apologising profusely for my past behaviour. I tried so hard to be the perfect daughter, granddaughter, sister, and auntie.

I reached out to my brother, confessing that I knew we had struggled to see eye to eye in the past, but assuring him of my love and willingness to help him and his family however I could. I tried to have a relationship with my sister-in-law, despite her being one of the most awkward, opinionated, self-righteous, arrogant people I have ever met. And I genuinely believed I had the best relationship with my mum—I adored her, would do anything for her, and tried in every way I could to make her happy and her life easier.

When I say I loved my family, I mean I absolutely adored them. I looked up to my mum like a saint, utterly convinced that I had always been the problem and ignoring how much it hurt to never be quite good enough, to always be "doing something wrong."

After a couple of years rebuilding, my grandad, God bless his soul, offered to help us buy a new home for me and my family—a fresh start for all of us. I was utterly gobsmacked that he would even consider this; it was a humongous gift. By then, Ryan and the children had moved in with me to my small three-bedroom new-build, and we were all living on top of each other. I was struggling because I had nowhere to retreat to when my mental health dipped. I felt constantly overwhelmed and stressed out, and my grandad genuinely wanted to help.

Not only did he help us buy a house, but he also funded a beautiful extension that turned it into our perfect family home—a space filled with warmth, laughter, and the promise of new memories. I was overwhelmed by his generosity; it felt surreal, like a dream I never dared to believe could come true. More than the financial support, it was the emotional impact that stayed with me. His actions made me feel deeply loved and truly seen, as though I had finally been welcomed back into the fold—fully accepted, valued, and embraced as part of the family once more.

That said, the generosity came with conditions. First, we had to buy a property within a certain radius of where my mum and grandparents lived to ensure we could be around to support them. Initially, we were expected to buy in the same village, but when we realised we couldn't find anything within the agreed price range, we were allowed to buy in the next village over, where houses were slightly cheaper.

Every decision had to be run past my mum first, who would then relay the details to my grandad. The two of them would discuss things privately and ultimately come back to us with a final verdict—either a yes or a no. Despite the life-changing nature of his financial support, I never had a direct conversation with my grandad about the terms of his offer.

Everything was filtered through my mum, as if I were merely a bystander in decisions that deeply affected my future. Looking back now, I can see this for what it really was: yet another layer of her control and manipulation. I was still being treated like a child—stripped of autonomy, not trusted to make my own choices or manage my own affairs. It was a painful reminder that, even as an adult, I was still viewed as incapable, still held tightly within the bounds of her influence.

- **My Gentle Soul**

There are no words that truly capture the depth of love and gratitude I feel for Ryan. He is the light that has pierced through my darkest nights, the steady calm that soothes my wildest storms, and my unwavering saviour. He is the most beautiful, gentle, and loving soul I have ever known. Over these past eight years, he has not only shown me what unconditional love really means, but he's also been the anchor that has held me steady when I felt like I was drowning in my own emotions. Through his patience and kindness, I have slowly begun to discover who I truly am—and what I deserve from life and from love.

Ryan has seen me at my lowest, in places so dark that I sometimes thought I would never find my way back. He has watched me struggle with the crushing weight of my mental health, felt the despair that threatened to swallow me whole. And yet, through it all, he has never judged, never turned away. Instead, he has shown nothing but unwavering love and genuine care. His presence has been my safe harbour when I was lost at sea. I've seen the pain in his eyes when I've broken down, the helplessness he feels when he knows there's nothing he can do to take my pain away—but still, he holds me tightly, offering all the comfort he can. That kind of love, the kind that stays when the darkness comes, is more precious than I ever imagined possible.

From the very beginning, Ryan has been not only my partner but also the most devoted and loving father to his children. His fierce protectiveness, boundless patience, and joyful spirit make him everything a child could hope for. He is their rock, their safe place, their biggest cheerleader. Watching him with the kids, seeing the way their faces light up around him, makes my heart swell with love and admiration. He puts their happiness and well-being above all else, always willing to sacrifice and bend over backwards to give them the best life possible. It's in those moments, seeing him as the wonderful dad he is, that I realize just how lucky I am to share this life with him.

Ryan hasn't just been a partner or a father; he's been my healer, my champion, my steadfast supporter on a journey I thought I might never complete. He has encouraged me to face my fears, to seek help when I needed it, and to believe in the possibility of a brighter future—even when I couldn't see it for myself. He listens without interruption, holds space for my pain, and reminds me gently that my feelings are valid. His quiet strength has lifted me when I felt broken and has given me hope when I thought hope was lost.

We have built a life together filled with love and resilience, even through the challenges and storms. Though we haven't had many chances for quiet moments alone as a couple—our focus being on raising our children and creating a home—I know that the love we share is real and deep. One day, when the time is right, we'll have those moments to ourselves, and I know they will be all the sweeter for the wait.

For now, I find joy in the family we've become and the beautiful children growing into remarkable, kind-hearted people. I am forever grateful for Ryan—the man who has shown me that healing is possible, that love can be gentle but fierce, and that even after the darkest nights, the sun can rise again.

- **The Rollercoaster Ride of Emotions**

I was 30 years old when Ryan and I came back together — an age I once doubted I'd even reach. On the surface, I was living a dream: deeply in love, part of a family that I cherished, finally surrounded by the kind of unconditional love I had longed for. Yet beneath that happiness was a storm raging inside me — a storm I didn't fully understand and felt powerless to control.

My emotions were a chaotic whirlwind, unpredictable and intense. I was a stranger to myself, still lost, still unsure who I truly was beyond the roles I played — the step-mum, the partner, the 'strong one.' I had no clear sense of my own likes, interests, or dreams. Instead, I carried a heavy, smouldering anger inside that often erupted without warning. It confused me — how could I have everything I'd ever wanted and still feel so broken? Why was life still so hard, even when love was finally abundant?

There were moments when the weight of it all became unbearable. I found myself needing to step away from Ryan and the kids, seeking refuge at my mum's house or, at one point, even a friend's caravan just to have a place where I could be utterly alone without hiding the depth of my depression from the children. I desperately searched for peace and healing, turning to spirituality as a lifeline. I meditated daily, repeated affirmations to train my mind to focus on gratitude, journalled every morning, and practiced grounding techniques to reconnect with the present.

Every book and teaching I devoured told me that I was in charge of my thoughts, that I could rewrite my story. Yet, despite all my efforts, I was still trapped — crippled by anxiety so fierce I couldn't leave the house, plunged into depression so deep I could barely rise from my bed for weeks, shattered by emotional breakdowns that sent me retreating into myself where I harmed myself in desperate attempts to cope. I hated who I was in those moments, a person I barely recognized and didn't want to be.

I knew I needed help, but it was hard to admit that I was still struggling — that I was far from the 'fixed' person I thought I'd become after leaving my ex. Why was I still trapped in these painful patterns? The only real difference was this: I no longer wanted to die. I had so much to live for — my children, Ryan, this new family we were building — and the thought of leaving them shattered me. No matter how dark things got, I couldn't bear the idea of putting them through that kind of pain.

The hardest part was knowing that Taylor, Laycie, and Ryan had to live with my emotional instability. I am so deeply ashamed that they witnessed me shouting, screaming, slamming doors, and saying things I later regretted. It breaks my heart to think that some of their earliest memories of me are clouded with fear or sadness. Laycie once told me that when I shouted, it scared her — and I have never stopped carrying that guilt with me. I owe my children a lifetime of apologies for those moments, and I hate myself for causing them that pain.

Knowing I was hurting them but feeling utterly powerless to stop was devastating. It was then I made a commitment to myself: I would find a way to heal, to regain control, to be the mother and partner they deserved. I dove even deeper into self-healing, immersing myself in the power of the mind and the belief that we create our own realities. I devoured books like *Breaking the Habit of Being Yourself* by Dr. Joe Dispenza and *The Biology of Belief* by Bruce Lipton, and studied the wisdom of Dr. Wayne Dyer, Louise Hay, and Esther & Jerry Hicks. Their teachings gave me hope — the radical idea that I could physically heal myself, that I was the master of my own thoughts and emotions.

Slowly, things began to shift. I started feeling empowered in a way I never had before. My outlook brightened, and as I focused on gratitude, blessings seemed to multiply around me. Life was getting better — yet the darkness still lurked in the shadows. Triggers would come out of nowhere, and in those moments, I'd lose control, spiralling into emotional outbursts that felt impossible to stop. But even then, I was different. I bounced back faster, felt stronger, and knew the way out more clearly than before.

This rollercoaster of emotions was exhausting, but it was my reality — a journey through pain and healing that continues to shape me. And every day I remind myself: progress is not perfection, and healing is a winding path, not a straight line.

- **The Therapist That Saved Me**

Determined not to let my mental health destroy the new life I had finally begun to build — a life with Ryan and the children — I knew I had to seek real, meaningful help. I couldn't bear the thought of repeating the cycles that had defined so much of my past. I wanted to heal — truly, fully — not just for me, but for them.

One day, while talking with a colleague at work, I mentioned my ongoing struggles. She told me about a friend of hers, a man named Carl, who offered therapy sessions from his home in Lincoln. By trade, he was a bricklayer — something about that really stuck with me. A grounded, working man helping people carry emotional loads that, like heavy bricks, were weighing them down. She explained that in his spare time, Carl practiced something called Integral Eye Movement Therapy — IEMT — and she described him as kind, approachable, and incredibly down-to-earth.

I had never heard of IEMT before. But when I got home that night, I fell into a rabbit hole of research. There was something in the way it was described — working with the subconscious, helping the mind reprocess memories — that gave me a flicker of hope. I wasn't exactly sure what to expect, but I decided to email Carl. I had nothing to lose, and maybe, just maybe, something to gain.

Walking into Carl's therapy room for the first time, I felt a strange mixture of nervousness and hope. I had sat with therapists before. I had told my story — or fragments of it — more times than I could count. But something about this felt different. Carl didn't wear a professional mask. He was warm, relaxed, and made it so easy for me to talk. And talk I did. I poured out everything — the trauma of Dunblane that still clung to me, the emotional chaos of my teenage years, the scars left by a controlling and abusive marriage. I was happy now, I told him. I had a good life. But emotionally, I was stuck — still reacting to a past that refused to let go of me.

When I finally paused, Carl asked me, gently, what I most wanted to work on. I told him it was the anger. The way it would explode from nowhere and consume me. The way it scared me — and hurt the people I loved. That was where we would begin.

He walked me through the process, then started the IEMT session. I followed the movement of his hand with my eyes, as instructed, all while holding the intense emotional memory in my mind. At first, I felt silly. Unsure. But something began to shift — not just the image in my mind, but the *feeling* that had always clung to it. I can only describe it as looking at the same memory through new eyes. It was still there — but the pain, the fear, the panic... it was dulled, less sharp, less consuming.

Something inside me lifted.

I can't explain *why* it worked, or even *how* it did — and I say that as someone who's now trained as an IEMT practitioner myself — but the change was undeniable. After just a handful of sessions, something that years of traditional therapy hadn't been able to touch... began to dissolve. I wasn't triggered in the same way anymore. The constant background noise in my head — that internal static of fear and sadness and rage — finally began to quiet. I could breathe again.

Carl helped me process and release trauma I had carried for over half my life. And not in a vague, abstract way — but in a real, measurable, tangible way. I could finally talk about Dunblane without my throat closing up. I stopped jumping at loud bangs. I didn't freeze up when walking into busy public spaces. The nightmares that had haunted me for so long slowly faded away.

It wasn't magic. It was healing. And it changed my life.

For the first time, I didn't feel broken. I felt whole — not because my past had changed, but because the way I held it within me had. I'll always be grateful to Carl, the bricklayer-turned-healer, who helped me start putting the pieces of myself back together — not as I was, but as I could be.

- **Something's Still Not Right**

Over the next couple of years, life finally looked how I had always dreamed it would. I was genuinely happy. I had been welcomed back into my maternal family and spent almost all my free time either with Ryan and the kids or at my Mum's. I had everything I had longed for — the most incredible partner, two beautiful children to share life with, the warmth of family around me, and a few close friends who mattered deeply. Life, on the surface, was full. And for a while, I truly believed I had turned a corner.

For the first time in my life, I felt supported — held in a way I had never known. I believed I had finally become someone worthy of love and belonging. It was easy to accept the narrative that the problems in the past were all my fault. I'd been told that often enough. I internalised the idea that I had been the one to behave badly, and that if I could just prove I had changed — if I could make it up to everyone — maybe I could be seen as "good enough."

So, I became everything my family wanted me to be. I did what was expected, ran my decisions past my mum, and tolerated the harshness of my stepdad because I told myself, *that's just how he is*. I justified my grandparents' judgement and control as generational. I silenced my pain when their words cut deep. I ignored the feelings of rejection, the moments I felt like an outsider in my own family. I buried it all beneath a fierce loyalty — because I loved them. And I was finally in their good graces. That meant everything to me at the time.

And the truth is, they helped me — especially in my darkest hour. When my marriage ended, I was drowning in debt, clinging to a low-wage job, and barely keeping the roof over my head. Then came the divorce — the legal costs, the settlement — and I had no idea how I would survive. That's when my Grandad stepped in. He was my saviour.

I still get emotional thinking about the extent of his generosity. He cleared my debts, paid off the divorce costs, helped me buy a new home and even funded an extension so I could give my new family the best start possible. It was more than I could have ever imagined. Over the years he had helped in countless ways — a car for my 18th, a deposit for my first home, new appliances when I needed them. But this was something else. He gave so much of himself, and I'll never stop being grateful. I believe now, with hindsight and love in my heart, that these acts were his way of showing he truly did care — even if he never said the words, *"I love you"*, in the way I desperately wanted to hear them.

But as I continued to heal, and as Ryan loved me with a gentleness I had never known, something inside me began to shift. My self-worth — once buried under shame and guilt — slowly began to rise. I started to see myself more clearly, not through the lens of old stories or family expectations, but through Ryan's eyes — eyes that looked at me with respect, tenderness, and acceptance, even when I couldn't extend those things to myself.

For the first time, I realised what unconditional love truly looked like.

Ryan never needed me to change who I was. He never judged my past or the chaos that sometimes spilled out of me. He stood beside me through the meltdowns, the self-harm, the dark nights when I couldn't see a way out. He has seen me at my absolute worst — at my most raw, broken, and lost — and still, he chose me. Not because I was perfect, but because he loved me *anyway*.

With him, I could be fully myself. I didn't need to hide. I could speak freely, be heard, and feel safe. That kind of love? It heals you in ways therapy never could. And it was through his love that I slowly began to understand that I was *not* the terrible person I had believed myself to be for so long.

But despite all of that... *something still wasn't right.*

Even with all the healing I had done — the IEMT, the spiritual practices, the newfound stability — my emotional world still felt like a storm I couldn't predict. The highs were euphoric, the lows unbearable. It was exhausting. The tiniest thing could send me spiralling — from pure joy to soul-crushing despair in a matter of minutes.

Family life, as beautiful as it was, often overwhelmed me. Conflict, no matter how minor, would throw me into a meltdown. I still had periods where I had to leave — to stay with my mum or a friend — because I couldn't bear to be around anyone. Ryan and the children would go and stay with his family, giving me space to breathe and try to pull myself back together. I hated that part of myself — the part that needed to run away. The part that still didn't feel safe in her own mind.

More than anything, I hated that I was modelling this for my children.

I knew I wasn't giving them the emotionally stable mother I wanted to be. And even though I had come so far, I still didn't know why I couldn't hold steady. I felt everything so deeply. Too deeply. When I was sad, I was broken. When I was happy, I was euphoric. When I was angry, it was as though fire consumed me. I didn't just *feel* emotions — I *became* them.

It wasn't sustainable. And I knew I couldn't live the rest of my life like this.

Desperate for answers, I returned to a therapist I had seen before — Debbie. She was gifted. One of the most experienced, intuitive therapists I knew. Her approach was gentle but powerful, and I hoped that with her guidance I might finally unlock the root of what still kept me trapped in emotional chaos.

She used hypnotherapy, guiding me into a deeply relaxed state. In my mind's eye, I saw a corridor lined with closed doors. Behind each one was a memory I hadn't yet healed — parts of me still stuck in the past, waiting to be acknowledged.

One of those doors led me back to something I had never truly faced — the sexual abuse I had experienced during my marriage. In that moment, under hypnosis, I saw it clearly for what it was: rape. I had never allowed myself to name it before. I had normalised it, even blamed myself — telling myself I had failed as a wife, that his actions were justified because I couldn't meet his needs. But in that moment, I understood the betrayal, the violence, and the violation.

And just like that, something shifted again. The shame began to fall away.

I emerged from the session feeling lighter, freer, more at peace than I had in years. I had released something I hadn't even known I was still carrying.

But still… the mood swings persisted.

I couldn't understand why, after *everything* I had done to heal, I still couldn't seem to live a peaceful, emotionally regulated life. I had done the work. I had peeled back layer after layer. I had found love, safety, and support.

So why couldn't I just be *happy*?

That question haunted me. But I was determined to find the answer — not just for me, but for the people I loved most.

PART 8 – EMOTIONALLY UNSTABLE NEW BEGINNINGS

- **Moving House**

In February 2020, we completed on and moved into our new family home — a moment that felt almost too good to be real. After years of heartbreak, upheaval, and survival, this house wasn't just a milestone. It was a lifeline. A space where the future could finally start to feel possible again.

The keys felt heavy in my hand — not with burden, but with meaning. This house was more than bricks and mortar. It was a sacred reset. A symbol of hope. Of healing. Of a life rebuilt from the ashes of everything I'd once thought I wanted.

We wasted no time laying down our plans — quite literally. An extension was always part of the vision. The dream wasn't just to move into a new space, but to *make* one, to shape it with our own hands. We submitted the planning permission almost immediately and began gathering quotes. We were fired up. Purposeful. Finally in motion.

Thanks to the incredibly generous gift from my grandad, we had the means to do it. That money wasn't just a financial boost — it was a legacy. It represented a belief in me, in us, in this second chance at life. I could still hear my mum's voice reminding me to protect it, to use it wisely. And now, here I was, pouring it into something real, something tangible. A future I never thought I'd get to build.

We decided a building company would handle the heavy lifting — the structural work — but the rest? That would be Ryan's domain. He was buzzing with energy at the idea. With his experience in the trades, he could handle building walls, flooring, fitting the kitchen and bathroom, finishing. But this wasn't just about skill. This was personal. Every screw he turned, every wall he reinforced, every cable he ran — it was love in action. I watched him, day after day, pour himself into this house like it was a living thing.

I'd catch glimpses of him — brow furrowed in concentration, paint flecking his skin, sawdust in his hair — and I'd feel something swell in my chest that I couldn't name. Gratitude. Awe. Safety. Maybe even a kind of reverence. He wasn't just building a house. He was anchoring a family. He was anchoring *me*.

Of course, it was chaos. Living through a build with kids underfoot, jobs to hold down, sleep deprivation, mess everywhere — it was relentless. But it was *our* mess. Our chaos. For the first time, the disarray didn't feel threatening. It felt alive. Like proof that we were moving forward. Creating. Building.

There were moments when we'd collapse onto the floor in the middle of the night, surrounded by half-assembled furniture and unopened boxes, and just laugh — not because it was funny, but because we couldn't believe this was our life now. A life we had chosen. A life we were shaping.

And somewhere in that whirlwind, something inside me began to shift.

For so long, I had lived in survival mode. Constantly on edge. Hyperaware. Bracing for the next emotional blow. But now, for the first time, I felt something softer taking hold. Peace. Or the beginnings of it, at least. My nervous system — which had lived on high alert for years — began to exhale. Slowly. Hesitantly. But consistently.

It wasn't just about the physical home. It was about the safety I felt in *him*. In the rhythm of our days. In the way he made me a cup of coffee without asking. In the way he took over bedtime when he could see I was fraying. In the way he listened — really listened — even when I wasn't making much sense.

There were still bad days. Days when old patterns flared up. When I would spiral into self-doubt or rage or exhaustion. But instead of collapsing under the weight of those moments, I began to let them move through me. And Ryan — he didn't flinch. He didn't retreat. He held steady. His love wasn't conditional on my mood, my productivity, or my ability to perform stability. He showed up for all of me. The wild. The wounded. The woman still learning how to trust good things.

That did something to me.

The rituals of our new life began to anchor me in ways I hadn't expected. Cooking dinner while the kids played in the background. Folding laundry while Ryan tinkered with the fuse box. Late-night conversations over floor plans and future dreams. It was nothing flashy. Nothing anyone would post about. But for me, it was everything I had ever longed for — not perfection, but *presence.*

And slowly, the tools I'd once used as lifelines — therapy, journaling, meditation, self-help books — became part of my daily existence. Not because I needed them to survive, but because I was ready to *thrive*. I wasn't patching myself up anymore. I was nurturing. Integrating. Becoming.

I no longer felt like I was clawing my way through life. I was learning to live it.

This house — this loud, dusty, half-finished sanctuary — was where I learned what it meant to be safe. Not just with someone else, but within myself. To be rooted. To be still. To believe, even for a moment, that I might be deserving of this kind of peace.

For the first time, I wasn't waiting for the storm. I wasn't trying to outrun my past. I wasn't afraid of the future.

I was home.

And maybe — just maybe — I was going to be okay.

- **Ryan's Diagnosis**

As we pressed ahead with our house plans, filled with hope and vision for the future, a shadow was slowly creeping in — one we couldn't yet name. Ryan had been struggling for a while. It started subtly: a constant heaviness in his limbs, persistent fatigue he couldn't shake, strange tingling sensations. Then came the pain — deep, burning pain that travelled through his body like wildfire. And then, the vision in one of his eyes began to blur.

At first, we brushed it off. Life was full and busy — the house, the kids, the chaos. It was easy to attribute his symptoms to stress or burnout. But deep down, I knew something wasn't right. I'd seen these signs before, felt them in my own body. Having been diagnosed with Fibromyalgia back in 2010, I thought maybe he was heading down the same path. But this felt… heavier. More frightening.

After months of waiting rooms, blood tests, MRIs, and anxious silences, the call came. A neurologist confirmed something we hadn't even suspected.

Ryan had Multiple Sclerosis.

It was a moment suspended in time — a phone call that changed everything and yet said so little. I remember the room blurring as he told me. I felt the words hit my chest like a punch. Multiple Sclerosis. Chronic. Incurable.

Progressive. Words that seemed too big, too cruel, for the man who had already carried so much.

I cried until I couldn't cry anymore. Not just for Ryan, but for us — for the life we were building, for the future I had finally started to trust. MS felt like a thief — one that had come to rob us of the peace we had fought so hard to find. My mind raced through every scenario. Would he end up in a wheelchair? Would he be in constant pain? Would I become his carer one day? Would our children grow up watching their dad deteriorate? Would he… would he leave me? Would this break him?

But Ryan didn't break.

He didn't rage or collapse under the weight of it. He took it in, breathed through it, and then simply… carried on. Not out of denial, but out of something far deeper — a quiet strength I had never fully understood until then. He still got up every morning and made the kids breakfast. He still found the energy to lay timber and hang plasterboard. He still kissed my forehead in the quiet moments and told me he loved me. The man who had every reason to crumble instead became my anchor.

Watching him face his diagnosis without losing the essence of who he was changed something in me. It shook me awake. I realised love isn't just about the beautiful moments — it's about the brutal ones. The unexpected ones. The ones where your whole world is turned upside down and you have to choose, every single day, to stay in it. To show up. To love harder.

That choice — to stay, to love, to grow together through something we hadn't asked for — was one I made with my whole heart.

And in that space of grief and fear, a new kind of love bloomed. One with roots so deep, it no longer relied on certainty. I stopped waiting for the day when life would feel easy or predictable. I started savouring the simple, sacred ordinary: his hand on the small of my back, his laugh echoing through the kitchen, the way he tucked the duvet around me at night without saying a word.

Ryan's diagnosis forced me to look inward, to redefine what it meant to be strong. I used to think strength was pushing through pain, putting on a brave face, getting on with it. But now, I saw strength in softness. In sitting with fear. In feeling it all and still choosing love. I began holding space for both the weight of what we might lose and the joy of what we still had.

And maybe, that's what real healing is. Not fixing what's broken but learning to live in the cracks — to let the light pour in through them.

Ryan's diagnosis didn't destroy us. It broke something open. It revealed a depth of resilience I didn't know we had, and a kind of devotion that doesn't need guarantees.

This chapter of our lives wasn't one we planned for. But it taught me, perhaps more than any other: true love isn't fearless — it's brave in the face of fear.

And in that bravery, we found a new kind of peace.

Lockdown: A World on Pause, Emotions in Overdrive

Three days after Ryan's life-altering Multiple Sclerosis diagnosis, the world around us came to a grinding halt. The first national COVID-19 lockdown was announced, and with it, our lives were placed on indefinite pause. The timing felt cruel — as if the universe had delivered one devastating blow, only to follow it up with another. Ryan was no longer required to go to work. I began working full-time from our bedroom. And the children —

confused, wide-eyed, and restless — were suddenly home with no routine, no school, and no real sense of why.

At first, there was an odd kind of charm to it. Like an unexpected snow day that lasted a little too long.

Ryan dove headfirst into the renovations, finding comfort in productivity, in creating something amid the chaos. The kids filled our days with puppet shows, living room dance parties, and Joe Wicks' online PE sessions. We wandered through the quiet beauty of our new village, hands entwined, trying to make sense of this strange new world. For a brief time, it was peaceful — like we were in our own bubble, suspended from reality.

But bubbles always burst.

As the days turned into weeks, and weeks into months, the pressure began to creep in. The magic dulled. The walls of our new home — once so full of promise — began to close in. Homeschooling turned from novelty to battleground. Work stress piled on. Ryan's physical symptoms quietly worsened. He never complained, but I could see the fatigue in his eyes, the strain in his movements. He was fighting a war inside his body, yet still showing up every day for the children, for me, for this house that now felt more like a cage.

And me? I was unravelling.

The early signs of emotional relapse whispered at first — snappy responses, tears I couldn't explain, restlessness. But soon, they roared. The noise in my head grew deafening. I felt like I was drowning in my own skin, like I couldn't escape myself. The claustrophobia wasn't just physical. It was emotional, mental. My mind was a battleground of guilt, fear, and shame. I hated the person I was becoming — short-tempered, emotionally volatile, erratic. The darker parts of me that I had worked so hard to tame were rising again, louder than ever.

When lockdown rules eased slightly, I sought solace at my mum's house — a place nestled within ancient woodland, its garden wild and magical. It had always been a sanctuary for me, a place where the world slowed down and the chaos faded just a little. Being back there stirred something familiar, something tender. I needed that comfort, even if it came with pain.

Because the truth was, my family dynamic was always complicated. My mum's love was fierce but conditional, often laced with criticism and emotional control. My grandparents — who lived in a small annex on my Mum's land by this time — had always been a towering figure in my life. Kind, generous, complicated. At nearly 90, my grandad was declining fast — depression and early dementia slowly dimming his light. And I still ached for his approval like I was a little girl again.

His milestone birthday arrived in April, in the heart of lockdown. We couldn't celebrate the way we wanted, so I blasted Stevie Wonder's "Happy Birthday" through my car speakers and danced like an idiot outside his patio doors. He laughed — really laughed — and for a few golden moments, I felt like everything might be okay. I needed him to know how much I loved him. That I was trying. That I was someone he could be proud of.

But even those brief flickers of joy couldn't hold back the tide forever. By May, I hit the wall. Again.

The breakdown wasn't loud — it was quiet, cold, hollow. Like a slow leak in my soul. I couldn't function. I cried until I was empty. I hated myself for it — for the mess I brought into our lives, for hurting the people I loved with my instability. I felt like a burden. Like a failure. I called my friend Pippa in desperation, choking on tears, and she offered me a lifeline — the use of an old caravan on their land. A little space, a little silence, just for me.

In that caravan, surrounded by stillness and the scent of farmland and trees, I fell apart.

I journaled every day, pages stained with tears. I tried to meditate, though my mind refused to be quiet.

I stared at the ceiling wondering what the hell was wrong with me. Why couldn't I hold it together? I had a dream home, a loving partner, incredible children — and yet I kept breaking. The shame was unbearable. I wanted to claw my way out of my skin. I thought about leaving. Not just the house — everything. Because maybe that was the only way to stop hurting the people I loved.

Ryan called me every day. He never guilted me. Never pushed. He just listened. Held space. His voice was a lifeline — steady, soft, unwavering. I cried to him, told him I wasn't sure I deserved him. That maybe he and the kids would be better off without me. He admitted that it had been hard — so hard — but that he loved me still. He reminded me that he saw the real me, even when I couldn't.

After a week, I came home.

The children ran to greet me, faces bright, arms wide. Laycie had packed a little bag for me with my childhood teddy inside — a symbol of love that shattered me. Tears streamed down my face as I held them all, overcome with gratitude and grief. They hadn't given up on me. They didn't see the monster I feared I had become. They saw their step-mum, still worthy of love.

That return was more than just a physical one. It was the beginning of something deeper. A quiet, resolute decision to stop running from the truth of who I was. To start accepting that my emotional spirals weren't flaws — they were symptoms. And they needed compassion, not shame.

I had survived the storm, again. But I knew I couldn't keep riding out each wave, praying I wouldn't drown. I needed help. Real help. Not just to cope, but to understand, to heal. And for the first time, I was willing to stop pretending I could do it alone.

- **Our Beautiful Baby: A Dream Realised, A Heart Laid Bare**

After months of emotional turbulence following the lockdown, on 5th July 2020, a ray of pure light broke through the storm—I found out I was pregnant with our precious Hallie Rose. The news hit me like a tidal wave of joy and wonder, flooding every corner of my heart. From the moment Ryan and I reunited, I had dreamed of this—of having a child together, our child. I already loved Taylor and Laycie fiercely, as if they were my own flesh and blood, but this baby was different. She was a piece of me and Ryan intertwined — a living symbol of our love and resilience, the final piece in the jigsaw puzzle of our blended family. And to make things even more magical, her expected due date was 13th March 2021, 25 years to the day since my trauma began, as if marking the turning point in my healing and giving me hope for a beautiful new beginning for me and my family.

But beneath that overwhelming happiness, a quiet undercurrent of worry ran deep. How would my fragile mental health fare during pregnancy? Would my struggles impact this tiny, growing life inside me? Would my medication harm her? Those fears gnawed at me, whispering their doubts in the quiet moments. I was painfully aware of my emotional fragility, and I longed for this experience to be sacred and untainted. I reached out to my GP immediately, desperate for guidance and reassurance. The kindness and understanding I encountered surprised me. Assigned a perinatal mental health midwife, I finally felt seen and supported. She explained how common it was to continue antidepressants during pregnancy and reassured me that both baby and I would be carefully monitored. That knowledge gave me a fragile thread of peace to hold onto, though the shadow of fear never fully lifted.

Against the backdrop of perhaps the most stressful period of our lives, the pregnancy unfolded beautifully. Ryan juggled working full-time while we simultaneously pushed forward with renovating our bungalow—trying to transform a cramped, chaotic space into the forever home our family deserved before our baby arrived. The pressure to get the extension built was immense. By November 2020, the building work had finally begun.

The excitement was tinged with exhaustion. My mum, fresh from managing her own annex build, took control of our project with a firm grip. Every decision, every purchase, had to pass through her and then my grandad, who held the finances. It wasn't how I would have chosen to do things. I longed for more control, for a say in the home we were creating. But this was family—this was the way things were done—and I swallowed my frustration. I didn't want to rock the boat, especially given the generosity making this dream possible.

Ryan found the family dynamics hard to navigate. Independent and experienced in the trades, he had a clear vision and a desire to contribute fully. It frustrated him deeply to feel sidelined, constantly having to seek permission like a child. I saw that tension in his jaw, the quiet clenches of his fists after long days. I admired his determination to keep working on the house himself once the structure was up—not just to save money, but to build something with his own hands for our family. It was his way of claiming ownership, of grounding himself in a future suddenly uncertain.

As my due date loomed, the stress became almost unbearable. We were living in a house mid-renovation—no roof over the kitchen, no hot water, no heating—right in the heart of winter. Hallie didn't even have a bedroom ready for when we were bringing her home. I knew she wouldn't need one immediately, but the unfinished spaces around us screamed chaos. The tension between me, Ryan, and my mum grew thick like a fog, smothering what little calm remained. I was still working full-time, trying to hold everything together, while Ryan pushed himself to exhaustion, building our future on nights and weekends, whilst suffering with a number of symptoms of his MS. I felt like I was drowning beneath the weight of it all. How much more could I endure?

Then, as if she sensed our need, Hallie Rose arrived 16 days early. On the night of 23rd February 2021, my waters broke just as I was heading to bed. What followed was a blur—24 hours later, I was admitted for induction. The labour was long, painful, and frightening. An epidural, then an emergency caesarean, and then Hallie didn't breathe for 6 minutes without help. It was truly terrifying. But in the midst of that storm, magic unfolded. When they placed Hallie in my arms on 25th February, the world snapped into focus.

The love I felt was unlike anything I'd ever known—raw, overwhelming, and utterly complete. It settled in my chest like a blazing fire, knocking the breath from my lungs and silencing every anxious thought. In that moment, everything else—the fear, the chaos, the exhaustion—faded away. I had her. We had her.

And suddenly, my whole world was exactly as I'd dreamed it could be. I had Ryan—my soulmate, my anchor in the storm. I had two incredible stepchildren who filled my heart to bursting. We had a home, imperfect and unfinished, but ours and full of promise. I had a family, complicated and flawed, but still mine. And now, I had Hallie Rose—our little miracle, a piece of me and Ryan, a symbol of all we had survived and all we hoped for.

Despite the fatigue, the tears, the unfinished house, and the relentless demands of life, this was the happiest I had ever been. For the first time, I wasn't chasing an elusive wholeness—I was living it. And that made all the difference.

The Emotional Tug of War

Motherhood became the crucible in which I truly found myself—sometimes searing and painful, but ultimately transformative. For the first time, I had a purpose so fierce it made even the darkest, most suffocating days bearable. Hallie Rose was more than a child; she was a lifeline, a beacon that pulled me through the storm. I woke each morning with a newfound resolve, a quiet but relentless determination to keep going, no matter how heavy the weight on my shoulders felt. Through her, I discovered a well of self-worth that had been buried under years of pain and self-doubt—a fragile, shimmering truth that whispered, *You are enough.*

It wasn't just about survival anymore; it was about living with intention. More than that, I came to understand how deeply my children's view of me—how they witnessed me being treated—would shape their own futures. I owed it to them, and to myself, to demand and embody a love that was real, unwavering, and unconditional. Ryan's love, the steadfast warmth in the children's eyes—these became the foundations on which I started to build a softer, kinder version of myself. It wasn't confidence yet. I was far from fully embracing my power. But there was a new, tentative acceptance growing—a gentle knowing that I deserved kindness, especially from the person I had often treated most harshly: myself.

Looking back, I knew I had been through too much—too many battles fought in silence—and I didn't deserve the pain or the harshness I'd endured. My mental health struggles suddenly made sense as a reaction, a call from wounds hidden beneath the surface, wounds I was only just beginning to face. It was around this time that I stumbled upon Emotionally Unstable Personality Disorder (EUPD). Reading about it was like looking into a mirror that reflected every wild thought, every desperate feeling, every chaotic behaviour I'd wrestled with for years. For the first time, I wasn't alone. I wasn't broken beyond repair or some kind of freak. This knowledge gave me something precious: compassion. Compassion to forgive the parts of myself I had once hated. Though I was never formally diagnosed, the insight unlocked a cage I hadn't realised I was trapped in—a prison built by shame and misunderstanding.

As the pieces began to fall into place, the questions multiplied. What had caused me to live this way? The trauma of Dunblane was like a jagged scar across my soul, keeping me stuck in a relentless fight-or-flight mode that poisoned so much of my life. But there was something deeper, darker still—an unspoken tension rooted in my family, a toxicity that lingered beneath the surface, like a silent storm.

For years, friends, therapists, even distant relatives had whispered the truth: my maternal family's relationships were far from normal. They were toxic, laced with emotional abuse. When I spoke of feeling silenced, belittled, and trapped, others saw the controlling and narcissistic patterns that I had been blind to. But I struggled to believe it. How could the people who had given me so much—and who I loved fiercely—also be the source of so much pain? It didn't add up. I convinced myself they loved me. They just didn't know how to show it any other way.

I knew my mum's childhood had been a hard one. She'd shared stories of always feeling "second best," a constant disappointment under the critical eyes of my grandparents. They offered no comfort or affection, only criticism and neglect. And yet, she allowed those same patterns to fester in her own family. My grandparents openly favoured my brother, their words sharp and cutting—judging every choice I made, every aspect of who I was. Their harshness left scars beneath my skin, wounds that never fully healed.

My mum's response was always the same: *accept them for who they are*. So, I did. I swallowed my hurt, bottled up my feelings, and tried desperately to love unconditionally—even when it felt like walking through a field of glass. But love shouldn't cut like that.

The tension was a constant undercurrent—poisoning every family gathering, every conversation. My mum's lack of empathy for Ryan's MS diagnosis was another source of silent grief. Because my aunt lived with MS in a way that didn't visibly affect her, my family expected Ryan to be the same. They dismissed his pain and struggles, making him feel isolated and misunderstood when he most needed support.

Ryan, quiet and steady, was breaking beneath the weight of their control. It felt like we were trapped in a dictatorship disguised as family loyalty. I was caught in the middle, torn between the desperate need to be the 'good daughter' who kept the peace, and the fierce urge to live my own life—with

Ryan, as an equal partner making decisions for ourselves. The pressure was relentless and draining. My mum's constant criticism of Ryan—listing every imagined failure—was like a thorn lodged deep in my heart. It clashed with the reality I knew: the man I loved, who gave everything to hold us all together, even when his own body betrayed him.

And yet, the people closest to me—friends, even other family members—warned me I was still caught in their web, trapped by their toxic grip. Hearing it from others was a cruel kind of clarity. I was devastated and utterly confused. I loved my family fiercely. They had done so much for us. How could I confront them? How could I choose between the family I'd always known and the family Ryan and I were trying to build? The guilt was suffocating.

This exhausting, soul-draining tug of war went on for months. All I wanted was one thing: a happy family, a peaceful home. I fought so hard to keep everyone happy, to be the glue that held us together. But it was breaking me, piece by fragile piece.

For the first time, I admitted it to myself: the toxicity of my maternal family was damaging my mental health—and had been for far too long. I could no longer pretend otherwise.

- **Strength in the Shattering**

In September 2021, the world cracked open beneath my feet.

My beautiful stepsister—my best friend, my fiercest cheerleader—suffered a psychotic break after a lifetime of trauma, abuse and emotional neglect. Watching her unravel, fighting so desperately to be seen and heard by professionals who only mislabelled, dismissed, or condemned her, broke something inside me. She wasn't just struggling—she was drowning. And no one was throwing her a lifeline.

When she reached her breaking point and tried to end her life, the devastation hit me like a tidal wave. How could someone I loved so deeply, someone I spoke to almost every day, feel the world would be better off without her? It tore at my soul. I was heartbroken—but also fiercely grateful she had survived.

At the time, she wasn't speaking to her dad—my stepdad. I asked if I could reach out and let him know what had happened. She agreed. I made the call immediately, hopeful—naive, maybe—that this moment would make him put pride aside, that he'd remind her she mattered.

But instead, I got a cold slap in the face.

A few hours later, my mum told me my stepdad wouldn't be contacting her. He expected her to reach out first. To give him permission to be a parent to a daughter who had just tried to leave this world.

I was stunned. Gutted. Speechless.

Still, I didn't argue. I went back to my stepsister—fragile and raw in a hospital bed—and gently encouraged her to send him a text. She did.

Her message: "Hi."

His response: "Hello."

No warmth. No urgency. No "Are you okay?" Not even "Can I come?"

Just one cold word that slammed shut like a steel door.

She was his daughter. His baby girl. She had just tried to leave this life. Wasn't that enough?

Apparently not.

I called my mum again, desperate for understanding. Instead, she defended him. Said it was my stepsister who had cut ties. That she owed him an apology. That he was right to wait.

My blood ran cold.

We were living in different realities. I could only see her pain. My mum could only see his wounded pride.

I realised we were never going to agree, so I begged her to stop pushing the issue. To not let this come between us.

But she wouldn't let it go.

Every call, every message, another wave of criticism toward my stepsister—how she lived, how she parented, who she dated. Every word was a stab, every judgment a wedge driving us apart.

I snapped.

I told her to fuck off.

I shouldn't have. I hate that. But I was shattered, and she kept stomping on the pieces.

She hung up. Texted me it would be the last time I spoke to her that way. Accused me of screaming—something I hadn't done. We dug in. I stood with my sister. She stood with her husband.

Then came the next blow.

I was removed from the family WhatsApp group. My lifeline to updates on my nieces—my heart dropped.

I messaged my sister-in-law, panicked. "We'll talk tomorrow," she said. That night, I didn't sleep. I was unravelling.

When she finally answered the next day, it was an ambush.

Ten minutes of verbal assault— saying I had been disrespecting my grandparents, that I was ungrateful, selfish, mentally unstable, toxic.

She even dredged up an old emotional breakdown—one I hadn't orchestrated, one I hadn't wanted— where I had gone to stay at my Mum's to have some space whilst she went to Germany to visit them, that she twisted as proof of my selfishness.

Her words burned because buried inside them was truth I couldn't deny.

I'd spoken poorly about my grandparents once.

I'd also fallen apart the day my mum flew out to visit them.

But none of it was malice. I hadn't asked to feel that way. I was just… unwell. Struggling. Raw.

Now my struggle was weaponised.

I listened, stunned, as she recited grievances no one outside my family should have known—ones she must have learned from my mum.

The betrayal burned hotter than the words themselves.

Ryan—ever my rock—sat beside me. Eventually, he stood and walked away. He couldn't bear the carnage of my heart being shredded.

When my sister-in-law finished, I snapped.

Years of pain trying to fit into a family that never fully accepted me boiled over.

I told her exactly what I thought of her condescension, control, and superiority. I told her to fuck off too.

Then came the next wave.

My grandparents emailed, sharing how disappointed they were in me and that they were withdrawing the financial support they had continued to give me. I'd gone too far.

I lashed out. Bitterly. Nastily. I told them goodbye, accused them of choosing sides.

I was hurt, angry, cornered. I hit back.

I'm not proud, especially not for how I responded to my grandad.

He had early-stage dementia. He was depressed. He didn't deserve my venom.

I tried to apologise before he passed in 2023, but the damage was done.

That moment became the final fracture in a family already full of fault lines.

My mum told me I couldn't contact my grandparents directly. Said my grandad was too fragile.

Maybe she was right. Maybe not.

But in that moment, it felt like punishment.

For weeks, I couldn't speak to her. Only text.

I needed space—to process, to protect myself.

She wanted to meet, to hug, to fix it—but I wasn't ready.

I told her I was done.

Done with the toxicity.

Done with the judgment.

Done with a family that only accepted the version of me they approved.

And then came more gut punches.

She dropped my children's belongings in our front garden just as we walked home from school.

She emptied her loft of all my belongings, every memory, every childhood item and dumped them in my garden too.

She emailed for updates on the house build—for my grandad—but wouldn't let me send them directly.

She sent a breakdown of every penny my grandparents had ever given me.

Then she asked to see Hallie—but didn't even mention Taylor or Laycie.

That was the final straw.

If she couldn't love all my children, she didn't get to love any of them.

Biology meant nothing to me—they were all my babies.

I wouldn't let them be discarded, judged, or made to feel less-than like I had been.

Not on my watch.

But despite everything, I still loved and missed my family—terribly.

As painful as it had become, I couldn't switch off my feelings.

They were my blood.

That bond ran deep—even when the people tied to it hurt me the most.

It was like seeing them clearly for the first time—narcissistic, judgmental, emotionally rigid.

Always in control.

Never at fault.

But clarity didn't erase love.

I would always carry love for them, no matter how much they'd hurt me.

Eventually, after many months had passed, I reached out to my mum.

I knew I couldn't face my grandma, or my brother and sister-in-law.

But my mum had been my whole world.

I felt lost without her.

For my entire adult life, I hadn't made a single decision without her approval.

She was my best friend, my confidante, my safety net.

Her house was my sanctuary.

Surely, I thought, love could outweigh the rest.

So, I tried.

I spent months gently explaining why I'd reacted as I did.

I admitted where I'd lost control.

I owned where I was wrong.

But I couldn't carry the full weight of blame anymore—not like before.

This time, I needed to be heard.

I opened up about the pain I carried from childhood.

How my stepdad made me feel small, unwelcome—like an unwanted guest in his family.

How my brother looked down on me, enjoyed poking my sensitivity to get a rise out of me.

The constant criticisms from my grandparents—that I was too much, too loud, too emotional, too clingy, too sensitive.

I was never enough.

Or rather, I was always too much.

I even tried—carefully—to talk about her.

How I'd felt controlled by her in my adult life.

How painful it was to hear her speak so negatively about Ryan, when he'd done nothing but love and support us all.

I thought if she could understand the pain beneath my reactions—

If she could hear what I'd endured—

Maybe there'd be compassion. Accountability. Healing.

But my words met defensiveness.

Criticism.

Accusations.

Instead of hearing me, she accused me of calling her a terrible mother.

She dismissed everything as untrue or exaggerated.

Reminded me, repeatedly, that she was the only one who'd always been there for me.

That she deserved loyalty and gratitude—not blame.

Maybe that was true.

She had always been there.

But being there isn't the same as truly seeing someone.

I needed her to know I wasn't attacking her—I was begging to be understood.

I gave examples.

How it felt to be branded "an arsehole" for my teenage mental health struggles.

How my grandparents repeatedly told me my brother was the favourite—and how that shaped my self-worth.

I wasn't making it up.

I was sharing my truth.

My lived experience.

But still, she wouldn't hear me.

And then—in a moment of pain and frustration—I called her a narcissist.

It was a terrible thing to say.

I regret it deeply.

I knew, the moment it left my lips, there'd be no going back.

No forgiveness.

Because if there's one thing I've learned about narcissists, it's that they never allow themselves to be called out.

They never accept blame.

Never take accountability.

Never let criticism stick.

Whether or not my mum is a clinical narcissist, that's exactly how she showed up for me.

Every attempt I made to express my feelings was turned on me.

I was the villain.

The unstable one.

The ungrateful one.

The liar.

All I ever wanted—desperately—was to be heard.

To be seen.

To feel like my pain mattered.

But in that family, my pain was always too loud.

Too messy.

Too much.

And so was I.

Acceptance

For years now, my relationship with my family has been completely shattered — a jagged fracture running through the heart of my life.

There were moments when hope flickered — times I reached out, desperate to reconnect, especially with my mum. I remember one call to my grandma. My voice was trembling as I spoke, swallowing my pride and pain to apologise. I told her how much I loved her and grandad, how deeply sorry I was for the ways I'd hurt them. I could almost hear her sigh on the other end and then came the words that cut deeper than any wound: I needed to do serious work on myself before anyone in the family would even consider speaking to me again.

In that moment, I was once again the villain in their story. The one who had strayed, the only one who had done wrong and needed to change.

I ended the call feeling hollow — a cold emptiness spreading through me. I vowed never to reach out to her again. Trying to be heard by my mum or grandma was like smashing my head against a brick wall over and over. I was the only one bleeding, the only one left raw and exposed.

I tried. So many times, I reached out to my mum. Apologised. Owned my mistakes. Begged her—pleaded—for a way back, for a chance to be in her life, and more importantly, for her to be in the lives of her grandchildren. I told her how much it broke my heart not to have her near, how much I loved and missed her.

But every message was met with more attacks — sharper than before — reminders of all I'd done wrong, blame piled high like a mountain I couldn't climb. I tried to explain what it felt like living with emotional instability, of existing in a constant state of fight or flight. But it was no use. She made it clear: no forgiveness. No second chances. She even said it would be up to my children one day to decide if they wanted a relationship with her.

I begged her not to let this wedge grow until it was permanent, not to let one of us die with this silence between us. I poured out my heart in words I never thought I'd say. But she was done.

And eventually, I had to be done too.

Slowly, painfully, I began to accept the truth. Through my own words, through my own desperate, raw emotional pain—I had lost my maternal family. If I had stayed silent, swallowed my truth, maybe they'd still be in my life.

But in losing them, I found something I didn't expect. Peace.

Without their constant criticism, manipulation, judgment—without their poison—I've become a better parent. A calmer, more grounded version of myself. My children are growing up free of the toxicity I endured. They are free to be exactly who they are—not who someone else expects or demands. I no longer walk on eggshells, heart pounding, waiting for the next explosion. I no longer question my worth. I haven't been made to feel worthless or broken in a very long time.

Yes, I still ache for family. That ache will never fully leave me. But I cherish the people who are in my life now more deeply than ever. And I see clearly, now, that I am stronger, more resilient, and more in control without their influence.

It took years—years to reach this place of acceptance. Years to stop crying myself to sleep night after night, aching with loneliness. Years to stop reflexively reaching for my phone in moments of joy or pain, wishing I could call my mum. Because even now, after everything, she's still the first person I want to share my life with.

I'll always miss the version of her I believed in—the woman I thought was my best friend, my fiercest supporter, the one I imagined would always be by my side.

But I've learned this silence between us is the healthiest thing for me. For my children. Even for them.

Because no matter what I said or did, I was never going to be enough in their eyes.

I'm far from perfect. I'm fiery, impulsive, reactive. I've made mistakes—plenty of them. But my children will always know they are loved, wanted, accepted just as they are. I believe our job as parents is to guide, not to shape or mould them into someone else's vision.

I try to keep our relationship open and honest. If one day my kids tell me that my behaviour has hurt them, I hope I'll have the courage to listen—to own it, to apologise, and to change. I will never turn it back on them or list their faults to justify my actions. I'll show up, because that's what love looks like.

Raising my children without a family support system has often felt impossible. But I've done it. And in doing so, I've grown. I've become more self-aware, more in control of my emotions, more accepting of myself and others. The anger that used to simmer just beneath my skin has settled. The pot isn't boiling over anymore.

I feel free.

Life without my family carries a sadness I can't ignore. There will always be a part of me that wishes things had been different. But now I see them clearly for who they truly are. What truly matters to them. And I know they will never change.

To them, I will always be the villain.

They believe I took my grandad's money while secretly hating him—when the truth is, I adored him. I adored all of them. I genuinely tried to be the daughter, granddaughter, and sister they wanted me to be.

Yes, I can be criticised for accepting financial help and then later lashing out. That was wrong. But I never asked for their money. I never wanted to be controlled by it. I just wanted love. Understanding. A relationship built on something real.

But in their eyes, I was always a money-hungry, ungrateful problem.

Money became their weapon—to manipulate, threaten, control. I lost count of how many times someone was warned they might be cut out of my grandparents' will for speaking up, for having a different opinion, for stepping out of line.

I remember my mum and brother having a political argument once, and my grandparents threatening to leave him nothing because he upset her.

Respect was treated like a transaction in our family. Do as you're told—or be cut off. Be who we want you to be—or you're out.

I never wanted to play that game. All I ever wanted was to be accepted. As I am.

I realise now that will never happen.

I can't change their story about me. I will always be the villain in their version.

But I'm no longer trying to rewrite their narrative.

Instead, I'm writing my own.

One where I am good. Kind. Loving. A mother doing her best. A woman who is healing. A human who is learning.

And finally—finally—I believe I am enough.

PART 9 - EMOTIONALLY STABLE MUMMA?

- **Becoming Emotionally Stable**

Throughout the ongoing conflict with my family, my mental health took a brutal and relentless battering. Piece by piece, everything I had once held up as evidence of my worth—my strength, my fire, my honesty—was turned against me. What had once been my light became ammunition in their narrative. My voice, once praised for its bravery, was now framed as defiance. My emotions, once seen as passion, were now dismissed as volatility. I wasn't a person struggling; I was a problem to be managed.

There was no room for grace. No space for the rawness of what I was going through. Compassion was absent, replaced by judgement dressed as tough love. Again and again, I was told that I should know better. That I was too old to be acting this way. That being mentally ill wasn't a reason—it was an excuse. I was too much, too sensitive, too unstable.

When I tried to explain the grip emotional instability had on me, my mum replied that she had "read up on it," but still couldn't see how it explained anything. That one sentence cut deeper than she'll ever know. Years of suffering, of fighting through chaos inside my head, of trying to survive without the tools I needed, were dismissed in a heartbeat. I wanted her to see the reality behind my reactions—that I wasn't in control when I was triggered, that I wasn't calculating or malicious. I was afraid. I was in survival mode. I was trying to hold myself together with trembling hands.

All I ever wanted was understanding. Not absolution. Not a free pass. Just a moment of, *"I see why you're hurting."* I needed someone to look past my reactions and see the scared little girl inside me—the one who never felt fully loved, never felt quite good enough, and never truly felt safe in the one place that was meant to offer unconditional safety: her family.

But instead of being held, I was handed blame. The pain consumed me until it became my only language. I began to truly believe I was the villain in my own story. Maybe they were right. Maybe I was impossible to love. I mentally replayed every mistake I had ever made—every outburst, every tear-streaked argument, every time I had begged to be heard—and turned each one into evidence against myself. Self-hatred settled in my bones. I grieved for the mother I thought I had. I grieved for the version of her who I believed understood me, supported me, loved me without condition. That person died in my heart long before she ever physically would.

When my Grandad passed away in 2023, it shattered whatever strength I had left. Grief didn't knock gently—it crashed into me like a tidal wave, dragging every unresolved emotion to the surface. The guilt was unbearable. I hadn't said goodbye. I hadn't made peace. I hadn't thanked him for all the ways he'd quietly held me when no one else did. The sorrow pressed down on me like a weight I couldn't shake. I stopped functioning. Work became impossible. Even getting out of bed felt insurmountable. Life had lost its colour, its meaning. Everything just hurt.

And yet, from that darkness, something began to shift. I started reaching for help—not out of hope, but out of desperation. I was under the care of a psychiatrist by then, and for the first time, I heard words that didn't make me feel broken. I was told I had traits of emotional instability. And just like that, a door opened. I wasn't attention-seeking. I wasn't manipulative. I wasn't too much. I was struggling—and finally, someone saw it for what it was.

Medication became a lifeline. Antipsychotics helped stabilise the chaos inside my brain. The difference wasn't instant, but it was profound.

Gradually, the relentless highs and lows evened out. The storm clouds parted, even if only slightly. I still had bad days. The depression didn't vanish. The anxiety still whispered. But the waves didn't drown me anymore. I had something I hadn't felt in years: control.

And with that control came transformation.

Through therapy, medication, and genuine support, I slowly stepped into the version of myself I had longed to be. I wasn't perfect—I never will be—but I was learning. My reactions became responses. My anger transformed into introspection. I could breathe through the discomfort instead of exploding from it. I stopped needing to defend myself constantly because I began to understand that I was worth defending. I started to *like* who I was becoming.

I became a better mother. Not because I did everything right, but because I was present. Calmer. Softer. I listened more and judged less. I created the kind of home I had always craved—one where my children could cry without shame, speak without fear, and be loved without condition. I let them be messy, be loud, be real. I didn't need to be the perfect parent. I just needed to be a safe one. With every gentle response and every repair after a hard moment, I felt the cycle breaking.

The deeper I went in therapy, the more truth I uncovered. In 2024, I attended training on child sexual abuse—and that's when everything I thought I knew about my past cracked open. What happened with the bus driver, with my brother's friend—it wasn't a teenage mistake. It wasn't me being promiscuous. It was abuse. Full stop.

That realisation hit with a mix of horror and relief. For years, I had carried the shame, internalised the guilt. I had believed I was dirty, shameful, that I had somehow invited it. But that day, I saw myself through a new lens. I saw a vulnerable child, aching to be seen, starved of affection, who had been preyed on by adults who should have known better. My heart broke for her. But for the first time, I also held her hand.

And suddenly, so many things began to make sense.

Why I ended up with my ex-husband. Why I tolerated the manipulation, the coercion, the sexual abuse. Why I stayed. He was the physical embodiment of every lie I had ever believed about myself. He confirmed my worthlessness. He weaponised my longing to be loved. I thought pain was the price of affection. I didn't know there was any other way.

And I finally saw why I had clung so desperately to my maternal family. I wasn't just seeking connection—I was begging for unconditional love. I wanted the kind of love that didn't require me to shrink or shape-shift. But I was asking people who didn't know how to give it. And when I finally experienced that kind of love—from Ryan, from my dad's side, from a few soul-deep friends—I realised how empty the rest had been. These people didn't love me *in spite* of my flaws. They loved me *with* them. They didn't ask me to apologise for who I was. They stayed because of it.

That's when healing really began—not just survival, but *healing*. I began standing in the truth of who I am: messy, emotional, fiery, but deeply loving and endlessly worthy of love in return.

Becoming emotionally stable didn't mean becoming emotionless. It didn't mean suppressing my fire. It meant learning how to hold myself through the chaos without letting it consume me. It meant learning to *feel* without *falling apart*. It meant no longer letting other people's perception of me dictate my own self-worth.

I know now that I was never too much. I was simply hurt. I was never broken beyond repair—I just needed better tools. And now, I choose those tools consciously. I choose gentleness. I choose grace. I choose truth. I choose *me*.

And that, more than anything, makes me one hell of a stable Mumma.

- **Moving Forward: Self-Discovery and Healing**

Healing isn't a straight line—it's a slow, often painful unravelling of everything I thought I was, and a steady rebuilding of everything I truly am. Through this journey, I've come to know myself in ways I once believed were out of reach. I'm not perfect, not even close. There's still work to do, wounds to tend, growth to chase. But now, I walk forward instead of stumbling through the dark. With each step, I reclaim parts of myself I thought I had lost forever.

For the first time in my life, I am emotionally stable in a way that used to feel impossible.

The destructive coping mechanisms that once consumed me—self-harm, suicidal ideation, desperate attempts to escape my own life—no longer hold power over me. The urge to disappear, to numb the pain in ways that only deepened it, has loosened its grip. The chaos that used to erupt inside me like wildfire—the explosive anger, the unpredictability, the overwhelming emotional storms—has calmed. There is still weather inside me, but now I can ride it out. I have learned to pause. To breathe. To witness my feelings before they become actions. I have learned the difference between reaction and response.

And that difference has changed everything.

As a mother, the shift is undeniable. My children no longer have to tiptoe around my moods or carry the weight of my emotional instability don't have to wonder if I'm really present or watch me disappear behind a closed door to cope. They see me *here*—grounded, steady, and loving. They see a mother who can sit with them in their big feelings because she's finally learning to sit with her own. I don't parent from fear anymore—I parent from connection. From intention. From love.

As a partner, I've softened. I've stopped expecting Ryan to rescue me or to make up for the love I didn't receive in the past. I can finally *see* him—not through the lens of old wounds or mistrust, but through the clarity of my healing. He has never stopped showing up for me, even when I couldn't show up for myself. And now, I meet his love with open hands instead of guarded walls. Our relationship has deepened, not because it's perfect, but because *I* have changed. There is room now for tenderness, for truth, for trust.

As a daughter, I've begun to rebuild something real with my dad. Not something based on obligation or filtered through the pain of my past, but something honest. Something human. We've found a rhythm that isn't dictated by old family narratives. We see each other now—flawed, but trying. And that, in itself, feels like a victory.

But perhaps the greatest shift has happened within myself.

I have become someone I never believed I had the capacity to be. A woman who is calm. Grounded. Kind. Compassionate, not only toward others—but toward herself. I no longer feel like a prisoner inside my own mind. I am no longer in a daily war with my emotions. I've learned to coexist with them, to hear what they are trying to tell me, to let them move through me without destroying everything in their path.

This healing journey has been the most gruelling, gut-wrenching, soul-shifting experience of my life. It demanded everything from me—every belief I had about myself, every attachment, every wound I had buried. But it also gave me everything. I had to let go of the relationships that were killing me slowly, piece by piece. I had to accept that some forms of love—even from family—aren't love at all. I had to walk away in order to come home to myself.

And in doing so, I ended the cycle.

The generational trauma stops here. I refuse to pass it on. I won't let my children inherit the same emotional silence, the same shame, the same fear of not being enough. I want them to know what safety feels like—not just physically, but emotionally. I want them to grow up knowing that love doesn't have to hurt, and that being fully themselves will never cost them their place in my heart.

And if I ever fall short—and I will—I will meet them with humility. I will apologise. I will listen. I will repair. Because that is what healing looks like. That is what love does.

For the first time, I know who I am.

I know what I love. I know what I value. I've found my voice—unapologetically loud, sometimes trembling, but always mine. I've found my style, my passions, my rhythm. I've stopped trying to fit into boxes I was never meant to occupy. I no longer water myself down to be digestible. I no longer dim my light to make others comfortable.

I am emotional. I am sensitive. I am outspoken. And I am proud of all of it.

I like who I am. And not just in moments of success or strength—but in the quiet, messy, in-between moments too. I'm proud of who I'm becoming. I'm not perfect, but I am intentional. I am a good mum. A loyal and loving partner. A friend who shows up with truth and tenderness. I bring warmth, safety, and honesty into the spaces I enter. And for the first time, I can see that clearly. I see the beauty inside me—messy, radiant, and real.

I don't beg for acceptance anymore. I don't force my way into places where I am not welcomed. I no longer let other people's discomfort with my truth dictate how I feel about myself. I offer others the freedom to be themselves, just as I have fought to give that freedom to myself.

This is what healing has given me: freedom, peace, and a fierce, unwavering self-love.

A love that no one can take away from me ever again.

This is who I was always meant to be.

- **My Chosen Family**

This journey I've walked—through heartbreak, trauma, and rebirth—has not been a solitary one. I used to believe I had to do it all alone, that survival meant carrying everything myself. But over time, I've come to realise something far more powerful: I was never meant to walk this road without others. My path has been illuminated, again and again, by people who chose me—who saw me at my worst and stayed. Some were only meant to walk beside me for a chapter. Others have become permanent fixtures in my story. Each soul, whether they offered love or hard lessons, helped shape the woman I am today.

The absence of love from my maternal family still aches. There are days I grieve it as though they died—because in many ways, they did. That kind of estrangement leaves ghosts behind. But what I lost in one family, I found—magnified and purified—in another.

My paternal family has shown me the kind of love I used to dream about. My beloved Nana and Poppa were the cornerstones of that legacy—gentle, loving souls who radiated acceptance and kindness. Their love planted seeds that have grown into generations of goodness. My dad, my aunt, my uncle—their children too—they wrapped me in warmth, even from a distance. I always felt it. Their love didn't demand I prove myself. It didn't require me to shrink. It simply was. And that kind of love? It heals.

My dad and I had years stolen from us—years clouded by bitterness and lies whispered in my ear by those who didn't want me to see his light. But I see him now. Fully. And in seeing him, I see myself more clearly too. The parts of me I used to resent—my emotional intensity, my empathy, my unrelenting heart—they're his gifts to me. His strength lives in my resilience. His kindness beats in my chest. I carry him with me, not as a shadow, but as a beacon.

Then there's Sabrina—my step-sister in name, but in truth, my soul's sibling. We weren't born into the same bloodline, but we chose each other. And that choice, made over and over, has never faltered. From whispered secrets at sleepovers to adult conversations laced with raw pain and fierce love, she has always been my safe place. My anchor. My shield. When the world made me feel unworthy or broken, Sabrina reminded me I was whole. We've weathered storms side by side, held each other through grief, and cheered each other through growth. She is a blessing I will never take for granted.

Ryan—my heart's sanctuary. Our love was never tidy or easy. It broke, rebuilt, and blossomed in its own time. We met as broken people trying to fill the cracks within us with each other. But love like ours doesn't fade—it evolves. Losing him once shattered me. Finding him again rebuilt me. Ryan has loved me through every version of myself—each one messy, uncertain, in progress. His love is not performative or conditional. It's in the quiet gestures, the unwavering presence, the steady hand on my back when I'm unravelling. With him, I learned that love isn't about being easy to love—it's about being loved anyway. Because of him, I feel safe in my softness. Seen in my chaos. Cherished in my truth.

To Molly—my sister in everything but blood. For three decades, she's stood beside me, unwavering, through every storm and every triumph. With Molly, I never had to explain myself. She's known all the versions of me, loved each one fiercely. She's seen me at my lowest, heard the ugliest truths, and never turned away. Her loyalty is my armour. Her laughter, my medicine. There's a kind of friendship that becomes a lifeline, and Molly is that for me.

To Pippa—my cosmic twin flame. Our friendship arrived like fate, not coincidence. She feels like something ancient and sacred—a soul I've known across lifetimes. In her, I found a mirror, not of my pain, but of my magic. With her, I can talk about the universe, intuition, trauma, and hope without fear of being misunderstood. Her presence calms me, grounds me, reminds me that healing doesn't have to be loud to be powerful. I wish she lived next door, because being near her feels like coming home.

To Michelle—pure-hearted and golden. Her presence reminds me that good people do exist. That warmth can be trusted. That not every kind gesture has a hidden motive. Michelle gives without expectation. Loves without condition. Her friendship softened edges in me I didn't even know were sharp. She made me believe again—in people, in love, in the quiet goodness of connection.

And then—my children. My heart, my purpose, my miracles. They saved me. They gave me a reason to keep choosing life when everything in me wanted to run. Their love was the mirror I couldn't look away from—their tiny hands pulling me back to myself. They don't care about my past or my scars. They just want me. Present. Real. Loving.

Taylor, my gentle soul with a depth of feeling and natural kindness that humbles me. Laycie, wild and radiant, the fire I once tried to extinguish in myself now burning beautifully in her. And Hallie Rose, the joyful spark that completed our family—a light that never dims, even on my darkest days.

My children are the reason I healed. They are the reason I rise. They are the reason I stay.

I never imagined I would live to see a life like this—a life full of connection, truth, and chosen love. But I do. And every breath I take in this healed version of myself is a prayer of gratitude to those who walked beside me—who loved me back to life.

Some people taught me how to love. Others taught me how not to be loved. And I thank them all. Because of them, I found clarity. Because of them, I found my voice. Because of them, I created a family not built on duty or blood, but on choice, truth, and unconditional love.

Because of them, I know what home feels like.

- ### An Emotionally Stable Future?

So, what does the future hold for me? Honestly, I don't know—and that no longer terrifies me. What I do know is this: I'm walking into whatever comes next with the clearest mind, the fullest heart, and a steadiness I once believed I could never achieve. The chaos that once consumed me has quieted. The war within has found its truce. And I am no longer bracing for the next storm—I am learning to simply exist in the calm.

I am surrounded by people who love me wholly and unconditionally. People who see me, not just for who I've been or what I've survived, but for who I am becoming. That love—real, raw, and unwavering—has rewired the way I see myself. For that, I am endlessly grateful.

Life is more peaceful than I ever dared to imagine. But peace isn't the end of the journey—it's just the beginning of a new one. I am still growing and learning, still unpacking the corners of myself that ache, still searching for healthier ways to meet the challenges that life throws at me. Healing isn't a destination—it's a practice. A lifelong commitment to showing up for yourself, even on the hard days. Especially on the hard days.

My therapists, Debbie and Carl, I hope will continue to help me dig deeper, to understand more, to grow into the person I know I can be. I've made peace with so much of my past but triggers still rise. Old wounds still sting. And now, instead of burying them or lashing out, I meet them with compassion, curiosity, and tools I never used to have.

I once read a quote—though I can't remember who said it—that's etched into my heart:
"Most people are in therapy to deal with those in their lives who won't go

to therapy."

That truth hits hard. If more people had access to healing, to emotional literacy, to safe spaces for self-reflection, maybe we wouldn't carry so much inherited pain. Maybe the cycles would stop sooner. Maybe the trauma wouldn't be passed down like an unwanted heirloom.

One day, I hope to explore DBT—Dialectical Behaviour Therapy—to expand my understanding of emotional regulation and deepen my healing. Maybe I'll eventually be able to manage without medication. Or maybe I won't. And either way, that's okay. Thriving looks different for everyone, and I no longer feel shame for doing what I need to stay well.

As for what more I could possibly want from life? Truthfully, very little. I have everything I once begged the universe for: a soulmate who sees and cherishes every part of me, three children who light up my world and ground me in love, a home filled with laughter and safety, animals who bring joy to our lives, and a chosen family who remind me daily what it means to be loved with no conditions attached.

I am no longer held hostage by fear or the desperate need to earn love that always came at a cost. I am no longer shrinking to fit into someone else's version of who I should be. I have stepped out of the shadows of shame, and into the light of self-worth. I protect my peace now. I defend my softness. I value my voice.

I know I'm not perfect—but I also know I am *enough*.

I am kind. I am resilient. I am loyal, loving, and brave.

I am a good mum. A nurturing partner. A trustworthy friend.

I strive to lift others even when I'm still learning to carry myself.

And that matters. That *counts*.

Do I regret how I confronted my family? In moments, yes. I regret the sharpness, the emotion behind my delivery. But I will never regret telling the truth. I will never regret standing up for myself and my children. I mourn the mother I needed but never had. I grieve the relationship I once believed we had—the quiet mornings over coffee, the phone calls just to say "I love you," the simple, soft bond I believed we shared.

But I know now: you cannot lose what you never truly had. And you cannot keep chasing love that demands you abandon yourself to receive it.

I will always love her. A part of me always will. But I love *myself* more.

And that love? That hard-won, fiercely defended self-love? It has built me a life worth living. A life I cherish. A life I fought like hell to create.

Brick by brick. Scar by scar. Breath by breath.

This is the life I choose.

Not the one I was handed.

Not the one I was told I deserved.

But the one I *built*—with my pain, my power, and my persistence.

And finally, after everything…

I'm free to live it.

Epilogue: The Woman I Am Today

Today, I am not perfect—but I am whole. I live with emotional awareness, peace, and authenticity. My scars haven't vanished; they've simply stopped bleeding. I still have moments of doubt, anxiety, and fear—because I am human—but they no longer define or control me. I meet them now with compassion instead of criticism, with tools instead of turmoil.

I am a partner who loves fully.

A mother who shows up, even on the hard days.

A friend who listens without judgment.

A survivor who has chosen not just to endure—but to thrive.

And more than anything, I am becoming the woman I always needed when I was a little girl: safe, soft, strong, and steady.

If you take anything from this book, let it be this:

Your past does not have to be your prison.

The pain you've carried does not make you unlovable.

You are not broken beyond repair.

You are not too much.

You are not too late.

You are worthy of healing, no matter where you begin.

You are allowed to rewrite your story.

And you are capable—so deeply capable—of becoming someone you're proud to be.

This is not the end.

This is just the beginning of everything real.

ABOUT THE AUTHOR

Amy Rose is a survivor, storyteller, and fierce mental health advocate. Aged just eight, she lived through the Dunblane Primary School massacre—an event that would shape her life in ways no child should ever endure. Over the decades that followed, she navigated emotional instability, trauma, misdiagnosis, abusive relationships, and the silent battles of depression, anxiety, and self-harm.

Today, Amy shares her story with raw honesty and unwavering vulnerability to help others feel less alone. Her debut memoir, *Emotionally Unstable Mumma*, charts a powerful journey through breakdown and breakthrough, offering a lifeline of hope to those who feel lost in their own emotional storms.

Now a proud mother of three, loving partner, and dedicated advocate, Amy is committed to breaking the stigma surrounding mental illness. She speaks openly about living with emotionally unstable personality traits—often labelled as Borderline Personality Disorder—while embracing a life of healing, love, and second chances.

She lives in the UK with her family and believes fiercely in the power of honesty, empathy, and never giving up.